# "WE BELIEVE IN YOU!"

## 12 Stories of Courage, Action, and Faith for Women and Girls

**https://historysmiths.com/We_Believe**

## Bonnie Hurd Smith

### HistorySmiths.com

**Please visit the "We Believe in You" page on my website for a special gift just for you!**

**https://historysmiths.com/We_Believe**

Design: Bonnie Hurd Smith
Illustrations: Linda Bryant

For more titles by Bonnie Hurd Smith
or to book her for talks, please visit
historysmiths.com.

# "WE BELIEVE IN YOU!"

## 12 Stories of Courage, Action, and Faith for Women and Girls

## Contents

## Bonnie Hurd Smith

### HistorySmiths.com

"What woman needs is not as a woman to act
or rule, but as a nature to grow, as an intellect
to discern, as a soul to live freely, and unimpeded
to unfold such powers as were given her when we
left our common home."

—*Margaret Fuller*

# Introduction

### Why Did I Write This Book?

In a word (actually, two): For you.

More words: Because of my audiences.

Still more: Because I think this book can be of service. This is not "just" a women's history book! It's a book about life purpose, faith, and courage—but you're still learning some women's history!

You know, I've been writing and speaking about women's history for roughly twenty years, and it's been fairly academic work up until several years ago. At that time, I started weaving more passion into my talks, more about what we can learn from women's history, and my personal feelings about the women I was presenting.

The responses to the talks and Unitarian Universalist sermons I'd been giving on women's history became even more well received as I became more personal.

Being passionate about Judith Sargent Murray in my talks came naturally after all my years of "living with her." My sermon on Elizabeth Peabody for her bicentennial in 2003 moved people. My sermon on Margaret Fuller, delivered during her bicentennial in 2010, resulted in hugs and tears. After telling Margaret's story, which is all about faith in action and life purpose, I expressed my hope that as she waited those fearful twelve hours for the ship she was on to sink that she said to herself, "I knew my life purpose, and I did it."

During the anniversary of the Civil War in 2011, my talks on women during the war, delivered in various towns here in Massachusetts, led in one case to a mother approaching me with her very shy daughter. "Would you PLEASE visit her school," she said. "The way you presented these women gave us all role models we didn't know we had because you make them real. You bring them to life. No one is teaching women's history at this grade level, and these girls need what you have to offer."

I don't know when I'd received a more humbling compliment. I was quite taken aback.

For me, history is very much a living organism. No way is it dead and irrelevant. The women I talk about are very real to me, and one of the reasons I love studying women's history is because these courageous, high achieving women have answers.

In history, we have entire lives laid out before us. We can see how and why women made the decisions they did, what motivated them, and what happened as a result.

Where did their courage come from?

Who did they have as a support system?

How solid was their self esteem?

What obstacles did they face and how did they get around them?

How did they make decisions?

How did they recover from bad decisions?

All of these questions have long fascinated me about successful women in history, but a few years ago, in the midst of a personal faith journey, two more questions presented themselves.

What role did faith play in historical women's lives?

How did they come to understand their life purpose and live it?

Not only was I in the midst of a faith journey after many years of squelching my own spirituality from a very young age, struggling with self esteem issues, overcoming the lingering effects of a painful childhood, dealing with "challenging" finances, not having the right support system, and the list goes on. While I was reading about these women, thinking about the role of faith, and studying with life and business coaches who all stress life purpose, self-care, and achievement, planets started aligning in my mind.

At the same time, as I stated earlier, my AUDIENCES were engaging with me in new and interesting ways during the Question-and-Answer period. THEY "got" the connections between past and present, how we can apply lessons learned to our own lives today and really get into some important discussions.

So that's what I've done with this book—connected those dots in three sections.

Section 1: Twelve stories from women's history. Each one of these women achieved great things for all of us, each one's actions were rooted in her faith, and each one knew she was living her life purpose.

Section 2: What advice would these women offer us today? I have imaginary conversations with each one! In fact, in this section's introduction, I tell you a true story about how much these women's achievements mean to women around the world who are working for equal rights, suffrage, or to end slavery.

Section 3: You and I have a conversation about issues so many of us continue to struggle with today.

The fascinating thing about studying women's history is that you end up feeling less alone. So many issues like money, self esteem, or how we conduct ourselves in the business world didn't get here over night. Some of these things have been generations in the making.

But the good news is that there are answers, and women's history is one place to find them!

And I really do want this to be a Conversation.

In fact, I've set up a special page on my website just for YOU where you can download a special gift or contact me. I hope you will, because these are important Conversations and I'd love to hear from you.

The link is:
Historysmiths.com/We_Believe

So…welcome!

And I do hope this book will inspire you to learn more about women's history. It's simply not being taught under the college level, and it's OUR HISTORY!

Please keep reading, taking classes, attending lectures, watching movies or plays, visiting historic sites, starting or joining projects, going on walking tours, celebrating Women's History Month (March), or talking to the older women in your family and recording their experiences —and writing about your own experiences and research findings. YOU can contribute to our body of knowledge, and it will add so much to your life, I promise.

Women's history is everywhere—endless, worth discovering, and celebrating for its power.

I was asked recently why I "do" women's history. I thought about it for a while, wanting to really distill it down to one word if possible. That word? GRATITUDE.

Women's history is a gift to find and share. I hope you will join me!

—*Bonnie Hurd Smith, Boston's North Shore*
   Historysmiths.com

Here is a preview of Section 3 where you and I have a Conversation about a whole lot of issues.

For now, keep some of this advice in mind as you read the stories of the twelve women.

And you can learn more about the coaches I quote here on page 266, the Coaching Resources section.

Enjoy!

_____

Historysmiths.com/We_Believe

# Special Section: Coaching "Shorts"

## Gems of Inspiration—A Preview of Section 3

I thought you would enjoy these "shorts," presented here in no particular order. Post them on your refrigerator!

Be who you are.

From life coach David Neagle: "Abundance is your spiritual right, it's the truth. Poverty is not. You weren't meant to just get by. God created everything 'whole,' not 'half,' including you. But we are raised to see lack, and not abundance."

What do you want? What do you really, really want?

David Neagle: "Your belief in lack will create lack in your life over and over again."

David Neagle: "What would your life look like if you didn't have to worry about money?"

Be mindful of the news and other media that come into your life. It's mostly negative, and reinforces the "lack" mentality that David talks about.

What would your actions look like if you expected success?

Others will fall down on the job and you will have to be
a leader and provider and step in.

When we are tapped into the four "P's," Purpose, Passion,
Power, and the resulting Profits, we lift everyone up.

In low moments, just keep going. ou can do it, whatever
"it" is for you. Have total faith in your ability to succeed.
Sure there will be failures, but keep the big vision in mind.

Don't give your power away to anyone.

You are goodness. You are here to spread goodness
and healing.

You are the center of your universe.

Do you react, or do you make things happen?

What are the lies you were told about yourself that you
know aren't true?

Enjoy the process of discovering, changing, and growing.

Stop questioning yourself!

Breakthroughs don't come from being logical.

You're supposed to offend some people! Otherwise,
you wouldn't be doing it right!

Life coach Baeth Davis: "If you are not for you then who
will be? ... Being extraordinary requires doing what others
are unwilling to do."

Tell the truth.

Question everything. Get your dander up.

You have the right to live on your own terms.

Don't buy into the status quo or messages we're told.

Find moments to replenish.

Self-care, self-care, self-care.

Tough situations are there to teach you lessons.
Remember that, and push through.

Guard your independence.

Stop micromanaging your life and let go of what you can.
Otherwise, you will burn out.

Life coach Christine Kane: "Mindset first. Skill set second."
Inner and outer are connected. Set the intention for what
you want, and move through the fear that will stop you.

Life coach Kendall Summerhawk: "The universe likes
speed. Money likes speed."

Actor Meryl Streep: "We are the sum of the people who
have lived before us … I am my people."

Author Henry Louis Gates Jr.: "Know thy past, know
thyself."

"I long to hear that you have declared an independency. And, by the way, in the new code of laws which I suppose it will be necessary for you to make, I desire you would remember the ladies and be more generous and favorable to them than your ancestors. Do not put such unlimited power into the hands of the husbands. Remember, all men would be tyrants if they could. If particular care and attention is not paid to the ladies, we are determined to foment a rebellion, and will not hold ourselves bound by any laws in which we have no voice or representation."

— *Abigail Adams to John Adams, 31 March 1776*

"... it is confidently asserted that every transaction of his administration is now laid before her — she is not only his bosom friend, but his aid and his Councellor in every emergency — and such are the energies of her mind, as to place her title to the unbounded confidence of her illustrious husband, beyond all controversy — several Gentlemen in Boston, whose character, and influence, are high in the political world — declare that was the President called out of time, they should rather see Mrs Adams in the Presidential chair than any other character now existing in America —"

—*Judith Sargent Murray to Epes Sargent,*
*2 October 1798*

# Abigail Adams

**(1744–1817)**

---

## Her Achievements

- Defined the role of Second Lady of the United States
- Helped define the role of First Lady
- First First Lady to live in the White House and define its style
- Showed "the world" an equal, political partnership between husband and wife
- Raised America's fourth president and guided him through his political career
- Through her correspondence, provided an eyewitness journalistic account of a pivotal time in American history

*(more)*

---

- Famously asked John Adams and his colleagues in Philadelphia to "Remember the Ladies" when they drafted the founding documents of the United States
- Ran a successful farm for decades while her husband was away on political business

**Her Story**

At a time when America was inventing itself, Abigail Adams defined the role of Second Lady, expanded the role of First Lady, and showed the world what a mutually respectful political partnership between husband and wife looked like. Although she could not hold political office, Abigail wielded enormous influence over her husband and everyone knew it. He relied on her judgment, her support, and her ability to manage their domestic and financial affairs in his absence.

Abigail Smith was born on November 11, 1744, in Weymouth, Massachusetts. Her father, the Rev. William Smith, the pastor of the North Parish Congregational Church, was one of the best educated and most prosperous men in the community. From him, Abigail learned early on to respect God and help others. From her grandfather, Col. Josiah Quincy, who had served in the militia and in the Massachusetts House of Representatives, Abigail learned the importance of public service.

Abigail's mother, Elizabeth Quincy Smith, put the family's Christian ideals into practice by visiting the sick and distributing "necessities" to those less fortunate. Abigail often went with her. At home, Abigail's mother taught Abigail and her three sisters how to read, write, and "cypher," meaning, to use basic math. Later in life Abigail regretted not having the kind of education that was available to boys, but this was typical of the time. In any event, as we would say today, she got the basics!

Abigail married an aspiring young lawyer in 1764 when she was twenty years old. Both Abigail and her new husband, John Adams, were smart, ambitious, and wanted to participate in public life. John rode the circuit for his legal practice traveling by horseback throughout Massachusetts, which kept him away from home for long periods of time. Little did Abigail know then just how much John's lengthy absences would become part of their lives. But she did learn quickly how to manage their household, finances, and their farm in Braintree, Massachusetts—not easy tasks, especially as Abigail started having children in 1765 with the birth of her daughter, Abigail, called "Nabby."

That year, 1765, was also when trouble between the colonies and Great Britain really started brewing. The Stamp Act was passed in 1765, initiating a series of taxes, repeals, and growing frustration on both sides of the Atlantic.

By 1768, John's law practice took him more and more to Boston, the state capital, and the family moved there, to Brattle Square. Boston was a tense place to be. British troops were quartered throughout the city to protect the King's interests and keep colonists in line. The climate was suspicious and volatile, so much so that on March 5, 1770, after a mob of angry colonists threw objects and jeered at a British sentry on duty, British troops opened fire and killed five men.

John Adams was appointed to defend the British troops, which he did, admirably, and it was the first time Abigail found herself in the position of having to defend her husband to family, friends, and strangers alike—which she did. She also had more children—John Quincy, Susanna Boylston, Charles, and Thomas Boylston, and the family soon returned to their farm in Braintree.

The Boston Tea Party of 1773 further fanned the flames of calls for separation from England. While many merchants and business owners hoped to mend fences with the King to continue the lucrative trade they all enjoyed, it eventually became clear to most people that a reconciliation would be impossible—not without sacrificing the rights as citizens the colonists had come to expect. John Adams played a prominent role in determining America's destiny, first in 1774 as a Massachusetts delegate to the first Continental Congress meeting in Philadelphia.

In 1775, when the British marched from Boston to Concord in search of the guns and ammunition hidden there, Abigail wrote to John, "Great events are most certainly in the womb of futurity." Her home was a scene of confusion, with American and British soldiers passing by on the street, stopping, and resting. It was possible her house would be attacked. She had no way of knowing, and with John in Philadelphia she was essentially on her own to defend her children and farm. That June, Abigail took her son, John Quincy, up to the top of Penn's Hill to watch British troops set fire to Charlestown during the Battle of Bunker Hill.[1]

Abigail's emerging role as John's eyes and ears was now essential.

## Independence

Abigail was burdened by shortages of money and supplies, and she missed her husband terribly. Members of her extended family were ill; some died. But, as Abigail wrote in a letter, her path was "not chosen but forever ordained," and that "'To Bear and Suffer' is our portion here." She also wrote, "The consolations of religion were the only 'sure comforters in the day of affliction.'"[2]

Americans drove the British out of Boston in March 1776. Shortly after, John Adams was appointed to the committee to draft the Declaration of Independence. Abigail famously asked him to "remember the ladies" in the new code of laws, and to abolish slavery. The men in Philadelphia did neither. However, Abigail's biographers all believe that she had at least some impact on the proceedings given her influence over John and the ceaseless letter writing between the two. On July 4 of that year, Americans adopted the Declaration of Independence, and the world changed.

Abigail's life on the farm continued to weigh heavily, but she was committed to providing the best education for her children she could. In 1778, John Adams sailed for France to negotiate an alliance between that country and America. John Quincy, age ten, accompanied his father, which made Abigail unhappy, but, as she wrote, she knew she had "once more discharged her duty to the public." Rumors of her husband's activities abounded. It took forever to receive his letters—if she received them at all.[3]

John returned home briefly in 1779 to draft the Massachusetts Constitution, on which the federal Constitution is based, but he soon returned to France taking his sons John Quincy and Charles with him. At this point in their marriage, Abigail and John had been apart more than they had been together. Controversy about John's activities continued, and Abigail found herself once again having to defend her husband. "When he is wounded I blead [sic.]", she wrote.[4]

In 1781, John was serving his country in Holland, securing loans and arranging trade agreements. Finally, at the war's end in 1784, Abigail sailed for Europe to be reunited with her husband and sons. She was there for four years, serving as a diplomat's wife and entertaining (and no doubt trying to influence) diplomats in London and Paris. As Phyllis Lee Levin, one of Abigail's biographers wrote, "Her ability to overcome obstacles surprised even her." Abigail also became exposed to new ideas, customs, and the arts. "Her horizons were broadening."[5]

But Abigail missed home. She missed the "Old House" at "Peace Field," and she was tired of her "useless insipid life." She wanted to know what was going on in America—the latest in trade activities, the development of towns and cities, styles of architecture—everything. Abigail was a fiercely proud patriot, and she wanted to be present. As Phyllis Lee Levin explains, "Whatever Abigail lacked in physical strength, she did not suffer diminished powers of observation. Her journal and letters reveal the full flavor of her reportorial gifts—and also her rabid nationalism … Three years after her arrival in England, this 'mere American' apologized for nothing, much less her impassioned criticism."[6]

Abigail also couldn't bear to observe the servant class in London and Paris—men and women who worked so hard just to turn over what they produced to the ruling Lord. She found Europe's rigid class system deeply offense.

## Government

In 1788, the Adams family returned home to Braintree. John had been elected Vice President under President George Washington; Abigail would be the first Second Lady, and she would define the role. From New York, the first seat of the new American government, Abigail wrote numerous letters to friends, family, and colleagues about the government and public policy. Perhaps there was "no other person" who felt "more interested in them," Levin claims. Abigail held her "levees" on Monday nights, which were a kind of open house where people could meet and converse with her on a whole range of subjects. She continued having to defend John.[7]

Tragically, in 1789, Abigail and John's precious daughter, Nabby, died of breast cancer. Nabby had undergone a radical mastectomy and never recovered. We can only imagine the anguish she endured during that eighteenth-century operation.

The following year, 1790, John and Abigail moved to the American government's new capital city, Philadelphia. It was an arduous undertaking, but Abigail was impressed with the education, conversation, manners, and dress of the (upper class) Philadelphia women she met. Abigail was still very much involved with raising and educating her children, especially John Quincy Adams who relied on her guidance and political opinions. She also guided the management of the family farm long-distance. John was quick to point out years later that all farm-related decisions were hers. Under Abigail's direction, the farm made money—and they needed it.

John's name surfaced as a candidate for the presidency when George Washington announced his retirement after serving for one term. Thomas Jefferson, John's former friend and now political rival, wanted the job as well. The 1796 presidential election was decided by just three votes, but John won and Abigail worried about the growing animosity toward her husband and whether or not America, just in its infancy, would unravel. Thomas Jefferson's Republican Party opposed her husband at every turn.

People now referred to Abigail as "Mrs. President" because many believed she had that much influence. Unlike Martha Washington, the first First Lady, Abigail was very involved politically. In fact, in a letter written by Abigail's contemporary, Judith Sargent Murray, to a cousin, Judith wrote, "Several Gentlemen in Boston, whose character, and influence, are high in the political world, declare that was the President called out of time, they should rather see Mrs Adams in the Presidential chair than any other character now existing in the United States."[8]

As Phyllis Lee Levin points out, "She had no recourse, no way of defending her husband's views to the world at large. Periodically she would refute bruising attacks by requesting members of her family to place in a sympathetic newspaper a letter or essay of rebuttal that one or another of them had written. Essentially, however, she was a warrior without arms or armor, a Federalist without office, a writer without a journal, a lecturer without a platform or audience."[9]

Among the issues that plagued John's presidency were his desire to remain neutral with Britain and France to avoid another war, and the Alien and Sedition Acts which were designed to protect America from excessive foreign influence. Both initiatives were unpopular, especially with John's "detractors" who hoped to prevent his reelection.

As it was, Abigail had not been a supporter of France since their violent revolution of 1789 when its leaders rejected all forms of religion in favor of atheism. A deeply spiritual, Christian woman, this government-sponsored rejection of religion was deeply troubling to Abigail.

Abigail also continued to endure her recurring illnesses, so much so that by 1798 she began to think seriously about her death and make plans for her children. Even so, in 1800 she and John moved to the "President's House" in Washington, D.C.—what we now refer as the White House. The house was still under construction, and so was the city itself.

Everything was a mess. Still, as the first First Lady to reside in the house, it was up to Abigail to set standards and establish an American style. Abigail had always been a perfectionist when it came to setting up her own household, and she did what she could, but she and John were only in residence for a brief time. Thomas Jefferson had won the 1800 presidential election, and in 1801 Abigail and John left for their beloved farm in Braintree.

### Retirement

After seven years of being separated from John Quincy due to his service overseas, John Quincy, his wife, Catherine, and their son joined John and Abigail in Braintree. John Quincy's career was really taking off. He had come to rely on his mother's political advice through her letters, and now he needed her counsel even more. He was elected to the U.S. Senate in 1803, and Abigail followed his career as closely as she could long distance.

The Adams' farm was doing well thanks to Abigail's management, but Thomas Jefferson's 1807 Embargo Act, which forbade American ships from trading in foreign ports, severely impacted the economies of every major seacoast city—including nearby Boston.

The next president, James Madison, repealed the embargo and appointed John Quincy Adams as Ambassador to Russia. In 1811, John Quincy became an Associate Justice of the U.S. Supreme Court. As a young man, like his father, John Quincy had studied the law and was an exceptional attorney.

Abigail was now helping to educate her young grandsons, including teaching them good penmanship. Levin notes, "Abigail's esteem for polished penmanship and for a literate writing style was certainly heightened by her own deprivation; young women of her era had received no such instruction, and she lamented this her entire life."[10]

The War of 1812 with Great Britain soon broke out. The British set fire to parts of Washington, D.C., and it was unclear if Americans would lose everything they had won during the Revolutionary War. But American troops resoundingly defeated the British at New Orleans, and the war ended in 1814.

That same year, Abigail's health was so poor people didn't recognize her. She could scarcely walk from rheumatic pain in her legs, but she continued to insist on carrying out any duty "to serve in any capacity, august or humble."[11]

Levin writes, "Of considerable significance was the fact of Abigail's endurance, her amazing recuperative powers, mightily reinforced by her abiding faith. She marveled at her very existence, at being permitted 'a longer sojourn' than she had ever expected, and this thought inspired her conviction that she was meant by some great design 'to fulfill some duty, to report of some mission or commission, to relieve some wants, to correct some errors, to soothe some anguish,' and, if she could, to 'dispell glooms' among her friends."[12]

Abigail wrote her will, and she and John "lived the last moments of their lives with humor, intelligence, and courage, above all … In her last days, she had a 'sense of energy' about life rather than resignation, still wanting the most from it," Phyllis Lee Levin wrote. Abigail was convinced she would live to see John Quincy one more time, even though he had been appointed Secretary of State by President Munroe and was now living in Russia.[13]

John Quincy hastened home toward the end of 1817 when he learned of his mother's failing health, and he made it in time. Abigail continued to rally to greet the many guests who wanted to visit the Adamses, but, finally, on October 28, 1818, Abigail Adams, surrounded by her loving family, died of typhoid fever. They buried her at the

First Parish Church in Quincy.

John, who was devastated by the loss of his dearest friend after so many years of separation, love, turbulent politics, and happy final days, described Abigail as "being equal in all the virtues and graces of the Christian life."[14]

**Her Faith in Action**

As Abigail herself wrote, "True religion is from the Heart, between Man and his Creator and not the imposition of Man or Creeds and tests."

Later, she wrote, "I acknowledge myself a unitarian— Believing that the Father alone, is the supreme God, and that Jesus Christ derived his Being, and all his powers and honors from the Father ... There is not any reasoning which can convince me, contrary to my senses, that three is one, and one three."

As the daughter of a liberal Congregationalist minister, Abigail did not hear the stern warnings by ministers in Anne Bradstreet's time about predestination, human depravity, and original sin. Instead, as Abigail's biographer Laurie Carter Noble puts it, her father "emphasized the importance of reason and morality in religious life. This simple faith his daughter Abigail confessed when she was received into membership in the Weymouth church on June 24, 1759."[15]

Time and time again in her actions throughout her life, starting as a young girl who accompanied her mother on visits to the less fortunate, we see Abigail's complete commitment to her "Path of Duty," as she called it. Her "duty" included defending women, the enslaved, and working people, asking that everyone be allowed to share the blessings of American liberty and equality.

She was here to help, no matter how difficult it might be. She was here to serve as a Christian and as a Patriotic Citizen, which for her were irrevocably intertwined.

## Sites to Visit in Massachusetts

Adams National Historical Park
135 Adams Street
Quincy, MA 02169
*The Park includes the house where Abigail gave birth to John Quincy Adams and the "Old House," where Abigail lived and farmed for many years eventually retiring there with John.*

Abigail Smith Adams Birthplace
180 Norton Street
North Weymouth, MA 02191

Home of Abigail Adams (site of)
Corn Hill (today's Government Center)
Boston, MA 02111
*Abigail's Boston homes were located near what is now Government Center. See the Boston Women's Heritage Trail Downtown Walk.*

Boston Women's Memorial
Commonwealth Avenue Mall at Gloucester Street
Boston, MA 02116
*The Memorial features Abigail Adams, Lucy Stone, and Phillis Wheatley.*

First Parish Church in Quincy
1306 Hancock Street
Quincy, MA 02169
*Abigail and John are buried here.*

## Resources

*Abigail Adams: A Biography* by Phyllis Lee Levin
(St. Martin's Press, 1987).
*This one is recommended by the National Park Service.*

Websites:
*Search for Abigail Adams at:*
Adams National Historical Park
Boston Women's Heritage Trail
Boston Women's Memorial
Dictionary of Unitarian Universalist Biography

## Notes to the Biographical Sketch

1   *Abigail Adams: A Biography* by Phyllis Lee Levin
    (St. Martin's Press, 1987), 58.
2   Ibid., 68.
3   Ibid., 103.
4   Ibid., 131.
5   Ibid., 154, 178.
6   Ibid., 240.
7   Ibid., 255.
8   Judith Sargent Murray to Epes Sargent,
    2 October 1798, Judith Sargent Murray Papers,
    Mississippi Department of Archives and History.
9   Levin, 334.
10  Ibid., 444.
11  Ibid., 492.
12  Ibid., 462.
13  Ibid., 479, 480.
14  Ibid., 488.
15  "Abigail Adams" by Laurie Carter Noble in
    *Dictionary of Unitarian Universalist Biography* (online)

"He is very saucy to me in return for a List of Female Grievances which I transmitted to him. I think I will get you to join me in a petition to Congress. I thought it was very probable our wise Statesmen would erect a New Government and form a new code of Laws. I ventured to speak a word on behalf of our Sex, who are rather hardly dealt with by the Laws of England which gives such unlimited power to the Husband to use his wife Ill.

I requested that our Legislators would consider our case and as all Men of Delicacy and Sentiment are adverse to Exercising the power they possess, yet as there is a natural propensity in Human Nature to domination, I thought the most generous plan was to put it out of the power of the Arbitrary and tyranick to injure us with impunity by Establishing some Laws in favour upon just and Liberal principals....

I believe I even threatened fomenting a Rebellion in case we were not considered and assured him we would not hold ourselves bound by any Laws in which we had neither a voice nor representation....

So I have helped the Sex abundantly, but I will tell him I have only been making trial of the Disinterestedness of his Virtue, and when weigh'd in the balance have found it wanting."

—*Abigail Adams to Mercy Otis Warren,*
*27 April 1776*

"We all have our own life to pursue, our
own kind of dream to be weaving, and we
all have the power to make wishes come
true, as long as we keep believing.

Let my name stand among those who
are willing to bear ridicule and reproach
for the truth's sake, and so earn some right
to rejoice when the victory is won.

I am not afraid of storms for I am learning
how to sail my ship."

———————

"Far away there in the sunshine are my
highest aspirations. I may not reach them,
but I can look up and see their beauty,
believe in them, and try to follow where
they lead."

—*Louisa May Alcott*

# Louisa May Alcott

**(1832–1888)**

---

### Her Achievements

- Best—selling author in America at the height of her career
- Supported her family through her writing
- Served as a nurse during the Civil War
- Suffragist
- First woman in Concord, Massachusetts to register to vote, and organized other women to follow her lead
- Abolitionist
- Temperance organizer
- Transcendentalist
- Advocated for (and practiced) equal pay for women
- Championed a college education for women

## Her Story

Most people, especially women, have heard of Louisa May Alcott because of her best-selling book *Little Women*. And, yes, her stories for young people were wildly popular and brought her fame and income. But there's a lot more to Louisa May Alcott. This high-spirited tomboy who produced plays with her sisters and wrote about their lives together in Concord, Massachusetts, was also an abolitionist, suffragist, Transcendentalist, the first woman in Concord to register to vote, and a hospital nurse during the Civil War.

Louisa May Alcott was born on November 29, 1832 in Germantown, Pennsylvania, to Bronson Alcott, a schoolteacher, and Abigail May, the daughter of a prominent Boston family. Louisa was the couple's second daughter, after Anna. As a child, before she could read or write, Louisa remembered playing with her father's books even if she didn't quite know what they were.

Bronson moved his family to Boston in 1834 where he opened the progressive but controversial Temple School on Tremont Street. The school was considered "progressive" because Bronson Alcott treated each student as an individual, opening "bud," who was worthy of respect and self-exploration. Educating children in this way is not at all unusual today, but it was in 1830s Boston. Bronson Alcott's book *Conversations with Children* shocked Boston parents when they learned he was teaching a more personalized view of Jesus. Worse still, he enrolled a young African American girl in his school and insisted on a color-blind policy. Many parents withdrew their children, causing Bronson to approach bankruptcy and close the school.

In the Alcott home, two more sisters, Elizabeth and Abby May, arrived by 1840. Sundays were filled with Bible stories, hymns, and family conversations about "the state of our little consciences and the conduct of our childish lives," Louisa later recalled. Long walks in Nature were part of the children's education especially after they moved to Hosmer Cottage in Concord, the first of many homes the Alcotts would occupy there. Louisa attended Lidian Emerson's Sunday school in Concord, meeting and being captivated by Lidian's husband, Ralph Waldo Emerson. He invited Louisa to explore his library, and she did![1]

Abigail Alcott was devoted to her daughters' education and entertainment. "I never went to school," Louisa wrote, "except to my father or such governesses as from time to time came into the family … so we had lessons each morning in the study. And very happy hours they were to us, for my father taught in the wise way which unfolds what lies in the child's nature as a flower blooms, rather than crammed it, like a Strasburg goose, with more than it could digest. I never liked arithmetic nor grammar … but reading, writing, composition, history, and geography I enjoyed, as well as the stories read to us with a skill peculiarly his own." The Alcott girls wrote and performed plays, made up games, and enjoyed the lovely girlhood Louisa later described in Little Women. But their mother also taught them every form of housework and needlework, which Louisa knew gave her independence —the ability to take care of herself.[2]

When Louisa was ten, the Alcott family moved briefly
to Harvard, Massachusetts, to join their English friends
Charles Lane and Henry Wright in establishing a rural,
model farming community called Fruitlands. As one
of Louisa's biographers, Joan Goodwin explains, they
would "make use of no animal products or labor except,
as Abigail Alcott observed, for that of women. She and
her small daughters struggled to keep household and
farm going while the men went about the countryside
philosophizing. In a few months quarrels erupted, and
winter weather saw the end of the experiment. The only
lasting product of Fruitlands was Louisa's reminiscence,
*Transcendental Wild Oats*."[3]

## Beginnings

The family returned to Concord, to a house called Hillside
near the Emersons. Louisa continued to read great
literature from Emerson's library, including Shakespeare,
Milton, Dante, Goethe, Plutarch, and George Sand,
among others. She began to write "thriller" short stories
she hoped would bring the family income—and they did.

In Concord, Louisa "got religion," as she would later write,
while running through the Concord woods early one fall
morning. As she described her experience, "A very strange
and solemn feeling came over me as I stood there, with no
sound but the rustle of the pines, no one near me, and the
sun so glorious, as for me alone. It seemed as if I felt God
as I never did before, and I prayed in my heart that I might
keep that happy sense of nearness all my life."[4]

But the family struggled financially. Bronson Alcott did
teach school in Concord and gave lectures on philosophy,

but he never enjoyed financial success. As a family friend described him, "Bronson Alcott was one of the most lovable men one could ever hope to meet, so kind and so wise, but he did not know how to make money, and as a consequence, when his dear wife's dowry was all gone there was no further source of income. Money meant nothing to him and he never seemed to understand why they didn't have any...."[5]

Louisa's happy childhood came to an end when Bronson moved his family back to Boston in 1849. There, "everyone" worked to earn money while Louisa kept house. She did work briefly as a domestic with a family in Dedham, which resulted in her story "How I Went Out to Service." Interestingly, the story was rejected by publisher James T. Fields who famously told Louisa, "Stick to your teaching, Miss Alcott. You can't write." Back in Boston, Louisa took in sewing, worked occasionally as a governess, and continued to write. As the editors of Louisa's letters wrote years later, she was now "charged with the duty of self—denial and the virtue of self—help."[6]

In Boston, Louisa heard Unitarian ministers Theodore Parker and Cyrus Bartol speak and she met Wendell Phillips, another Unitarian and Transcendentalist. She met the abolitionist William Lloyd Garrison, "and other great men," she later wrote. She would "sit in [her] corner weekly, staring and enjoying [herself]." All of these men, along with Emerson, provided spiritual support and guidance.[7]

In Boston, Louisa was able to renew her love for the theater and she made friends in the theatrical community. During the summer months of 1855 and 1857, she organized the Walpole Amateur Dramatic Company in Walpole, New Hampshire, where she stayed on vacation. Moving back to Concord with her family in 1857, Louisa quickly organized the Concord Dramatic Union. But she still spent most of these years in Boston, writing and sending money home. Publishing under the pen name A.M. Barnard, she found a market for her romance and thriller stories. "Pauline's Passion and Punishment," which appeared in an 1863 edition of Frank Leslie's *Illustrated Newsletter*, won her a $100 prize.

## War

These were the years of the Civil War, and Louisa, an abolitionist since childhood, wanted to do her part: "I am scraping lint and making blue jackets for our boys," she wrote. "My May blood is up. I must go to the front to nurse the poor helpless soldiers who are wounded and bleeding. I must go, and good-by if I never return." Later in life she explained, "I became an abolitionist at an early age, but I have never been able to decide whether I was made so by seeing the portrait of George Thompson [the British abolitionist] hidden under a bed in our house during the Garrison riot … or because I was saved from drowning in Frog Pond some years later by a colored boy. However that may be, the conversion was genuine; and my greatest pride is in the fact that I lived to know the brave men and women who did so much for the cause, and that I had a very small share in the war which put an end to a great wrong."

Louisa worked briefly as a nurse at the Union Hotel Hospital in Georgetown, Virginia, where she contracted typhoid pneumonia and was sent home. Historians believe that her health was "permanently damaged" as a result of her fevers and the mercury chloride she was prescribed. But after recovering, she penned "Hospital Sketches," which was serialized in the *Boston Commonwealth* and then published as a book in 1863. Joan Goodwin tells us, "the book was extremely popular and stimulated calls for more of her work." That December, Louisa published her first novel, *Moods*, and her dramatization of "Scenes from Dickens" opened in Boston "as a benefit for the Sanitary Commission," an organization that raised money and supplies for Union soldiers. But it was her thrillers that provided steady income—her "blood and thunder tales" that were "racy narratives employing sharp characterizations and cliff-hanger technique."[8]

## Fame

Louisa spent a year in Europe after the war as the companion of young Anna Weld, and her return to Boston launched her stunningly successful career as a writer for children. In 1867, Louisa was asked to edit and write for *Merry's Museum*, a magazine for young people. Thomas Nile, the magazine's publisher, asked her to write something specifically for girls. He published Part One of *Little Women* the following year, on October 1, 1868, and it was an instant best seller. As one of Louisa's biographers wrote, "Most critics found it sprightly and agreeable, and young readers began to clamor for a sequel." Louisa obliged. Part Two of *Little Women* appeared on April 14, 1869. The same biographer wrote, "Louisa May Alcott had at last found not only her style but her fortune."[9]

Now, Louisa was in demand and she quickly learned how to manage the media and her fans. Her reviews

were glowing. People wanted to meet her, secure her
photograph and autograph. Her fans made the journey
to Concord in droves, where she was now living with her
widowed sister, Anna. She was the most famous author
in America, her book sales even outpacing Henry James
and Herman Melville. To find a quiet place to write, Louisa
often walked the eighteen miles to Boston to stay at a
hotel. But it was her young admirers who particularly
delighted Louisa. As her friend Mary Bartol wrote at the
time, "She talks to girls and boys on their own plane of
life, colored with the robustness of sports and strength,
and while she grasps their hands, she holds before them
a lofty ideal. It is no wonder that they flocked into her
presence, whenever they had the opportunity." Louisa was
often called "the darling of all American nurseries."[10]

When Louisa returned to Europe in 1870, she was now "a
lion on a grand tour." In Boston, publishers tried to outbid
each other for her work, and she produced more books
and stories for young people along with autobiographical
works for adults. As Joan Goodwin describes these years,
"From this point on Louisa May Alcott was a victim of her
own success. Though she yearned to do more serious
fiction, children's books flowed from her pen for the rest of
her life because their sales supported her family. 'Twenty
years ago,' she wrote in her journal in June, 1872, 'I
resolved to make the family independent if I could. At forty
that is done. Debts all paid, even the outlawed ones, and
we have enough to be comfortable. It has cost me my
health, perhaps; but as I still live, there is more for me to
do, I suppose.'"[11]

Louisa also continued her political work during the 1870s,
writing for Lucy Stone's woman suffrage newspaper

the *Woman's Journal* and organizing Concord women to register to vote for school committee. She attended the Women's Congress of 1875 in Syracuse, New York, where she was introduced to a cheering audience by Mary Ashton Rice Livermore, a prominent suffragist, abolitionist, temperance leader, and former head of Boston's Sanitary Commission. She organized a temperance society in Concord, which she felt was "much needed." She advocated for equal pay for women and a college education because "she devoutly believed that woman should do whatever she could do well, in church or school or State." Edna Dow Cheney famously wrote about her, "Miss Alcott always took her stand not for herself, but for her family, her class, her sex."[12]

In 1880, Louisa's sister May died from complications of childbirth, and the baby, named for Louisa but called "Lulu," was sent to Boston where Louisa now lived. Louisa published the stories she told her niece as *Lulu's Library*. In 1882, after her father suffered a stroke, Louisa made a home for all of them at 10 Louisburg Square on Boston's Beacon Hill. Louisa herself was increasingly ill and in search of remedies and quiet places to write. She eventually found her way to the homeopathic Dr. Rhoda Lawrence's convalescent home in nearby Roxbury. Knowing her death was near, Louisa adopted her sister Anna's son John Pratt, entrusting her copyrights to him, and stipulating that her estate be shared by Anna, John, his brother Fred, and Lulu.

Louisa visited her father for the last time on March 1, 1888. That day, he said to her, "I am going up. Come with me." She replied, "Oh, I wish I could." Bronson Alcott died on March 4; she died on March 6 at age 56. Her family buried her in Sleepy Hollow Cemetery on Author's Ridge, near her beloved Ralph Waldo Emerson. Her gravesite features a Civil War marker. After her death, a group of women in Concord purchased Louisa's most famous home to restore and preserve it. Children from all over the country sent donations. Today, this home, Orchard House, is visited by thousands of Louisa May Alcott devotees every year.[13]

## Her Faith in Action

Louisa's family practiced the Christian tradition of generosity, despite their own poverty, helping anyone in need or who came to their door. This included sheltering an escaped slave on his way to Canada. The Alcotts, along with most of their friends, were Unitarians who also became involved in Transcendentalism. Louisa's life was marked by her faith, intellectually and spiritually. That lovely fall afternoon in Concord, when Louisa "got religion" running through the woods, produced an intensely devout girl who relied on God's presence in her life as an adult.

She wrote:

"Something born of the lovely hour, a happy mood, and the unfolding aspirations of a child's soul seemed to bring me very near to God, and in the hush of that morning hour I always felt that I 'got religion' as the phrase goes. A new and vital sense of His presence, tender and sustaining as a father's arms, came to me then, never to change through forty years of life's vicissitudes, but to grow stronger for the sharp discipline of poverty and pain, sorrow and success."

"In adulthood," she added, "when feeling most alone, I find refuge in the Almighty Friend. If this is experiencing religion, I have done it; but I think it is only the lesson one must learn as it comes, and I am glad to know it."

Her comment at age forty, "As I still live, there is more for me to do, I suppose," indicates a sense of the purpose in life she finally realized with the publication of *Little Women* and all the good that came from it.

## Sites to Visit in Massachusetts

Home of Louisa May Alcott
Hosmer Cottage
586 Main Street
Concord, MA 01742
*This house is privately owned. The Alcotts moved here after Bronson Alcott closed the Temple School in 1839.*

Home of Louisa May Alcott
The Wayside
455 Lexington Road
Concord, MA 01742
*Called "Hillside" by the Alcotts, the house is managed by the National Park Service and open year—round. The Alcotts moved here in 1845.*

Home of Louisa May Alcott
Orchard House
399 Lexington Road
Concord, MA 01742
*Called "Apple Slump" by the Alcotts when they moved here in 1858, the house is open for tours year—round.*

Grave Site of Louisa May Alcott
Sleepy Hollow Cemetery
Bedford Street
Concord, MA 01742
*Follow the signs to Author's Ridge where you will find
Louisa's grave site—and bring daffodils, her favorite
flower.*

Home of Louisa May Alcott
20 Pinkney Street
Boston, MA 02108
*This house is privately owned. The Alcotts lived here
when Louisa was a child.*

Home of Louisa May Alcott
10 Louisburg Square
Boston, MA 02108
*This house is privately owned. Louisa purchased this
home toward the end of her life.*

Homes of Louisa May Alcott
26 East Brookline Street
Boston, MA 02129
*This is one house where Louisa lived in the South End;
she and her family also lived on Harrison Avenue at Beach
Street and Dedham Street. She wrote the sequel to* Little
Women *from rented rooms on West Brookline Street.*

## Resources

*The Selected Letters of Louisa May Alcott* by Joel Myerson, Daniel Shealy, and Madeline B. Stern (Little, Brown and Company, 1987).

*Alcott in Her Own Time* by Daniel Shealy, ed. (University of Iowa Press, 2005).

Websites:
*Search for Louisa May Alcott at:*
Boston Women's Heritage Trail
Dictionary of Unitarian Universalist Biography
Orchard House

## Notes to the Biographical Sketch

1   *Alcott in Her Own Time* by Daniel Shealy, ed. (University of Iowa Press, 2005), 34.
2   "Louisa May Alcott" by Joan Goodwin in *Dictionary of Unitarian Universalist Biography*.
3   Ibid.
4   Ibid.
5   Shealy, 164.
6   *The Selected Letters of Louisa May Alcott* by Joel Myerson, Daniel Shealy, and Madeline B. Stern (Little, Brown and Company, 1987), xix.
7   Goodwin.
8   Goodwin, and Myerson, Shealy, Stern, xxv.
9   Myerson, Shealy, Stern, xxviii.
10  Shealy, 44, 30.
11  Myserson, Shealy, Stern, xxix, and Goodwin.
12  Goodwin, and Shealy, 69, 54.
13  Goodwin.

"I am obnoxious to each carping tongue
Who says my hand a needle better fits,
A poet's pen, all scorn, I should thus wrong;
For such despite they cast on female wits:
If what I do prove well, it won't advance,
They'll say it's stolen, or else it was by chance."

———————

"To My Dear and Loving Husband

If ever two were one, then surely we.
If ever man were lov'd by wife, then thee.
If ever wife was happy in a man,
Compare with me, ye women, if you can.
I prize thy love more than whole Mines of gold,
Or all the riches that the East doth hold.
My love is such that Rivers cannot quench,
Nor ought but love from thee give recompense.
Thy love is such I can in no way repay;
The heavens reward thee manifold I pray.
Then while we live, in love lets so persever,
That when we live no more, we may live ever."

—*Anne Bradstreet*

# Anne Bradstreet

### (ca. 1612–1672)

***

## Her Achievements

- First published American poet
- First woman poet in the "New World"—as such, one of the most important figures in American literature
- The voice for New England in Old England; her political poems in particular were written during a very turbulent time in England
- An early pioneer in the New World when she arrived in 1630; her poems provided some of the only documentation of women's lives at that time

*(more)*

***

- An early settler of three towns—Newtowne (Cambridge), Ipswich, and Andover (North Andover)
- Articulated what it meant to be an American, a mother, and a person of faith during "bleak and despairing times."[1]

## Her Story

Anne Bradstreet's poetry was the voice of early New England in Old England, the voice of a new country, and even a new era, according to her biographer, Charlotte Gordon. Anne's book of poems changed the way people in England thought about America. As Gordon writes, "Despite her modesty in life, [Anne] would be the star of a story that would be told for centuries, the tale of what one individual, even a person of exceedingly 'small frame,' could accomplish if she were brave enough, smart enough, and like the country she had helped create, boldly independent."[2]

Writing at a time when the act of writing would have been considered odd (as women were not viewed as intellectual beings) or even dangerous to a woman's health, Anne lived a life of faith and imagination believing her gifts to be God-sent and to be used for the benefit of her new country.

Anne Bradstreet was born in 1612 in Northampton, England, to Thomas Dudley and Dorothy Yorke. The exact date of her birth is unclear. Both parents were of minor nobility and well educated; they, in turn, educated Anne, the oldest daughter, her three younger sisters, and Anne's older brother, Samuel. Thomas Dudley served as a page to the Earl of Northampton, meaning, he was essentially the Earl's business manager. The Dudley's lived in the Earl's Castle Ashby, a place of sophistication, high standards, and high fashion.

Anne was her father's "favorite," and she was taught literature, history, and several languages. By all accounts, Thomas Dudley was a "force"—unusually intelligent, and a man of high expectations. Anne was drawn to poetry at a young age, and she and her father studied it together. It was clear to Thomas Dudley that he had a gifted daughter.

## Puritanism

In 1620, Anne's father took a new position in Lincolnshire as the Earl of Lincolnshire's steward. Anne spent time with the Earl's mother, Elizabeth, who believed strongly in female abilities. In Lincolnshire the Dudley family attended St. Botolph's Church, which was presided over by the famous Puritan minister John Cotton. The Dudleys were already a prominent Puritan family, and they welcomed John Cotton's vision of a land free from the Catholic Church in Rome and the Anglican Church in England—a New England, where they could forge their own society and practice their "pure" religion.

Anne was ten years old when Simon Bradstreet joined the Dudley household to assist her father. Simon was a recent graduate of Emmanuel College, a Puritan stronghold. He was genial, full of fun, well mannered—and a Puritan. His father, a vicar, had died when he was fifteen; his mother had died even earlier. Simon became as much a part of the Dudley family as he was Thomas Dudley's assistant. Simon and Anne spent many hours together discussing politics and theology, which Anne's father encouraged.

It was unusual at the time for a girl to express her opinions, but the Puritans were under attack. Anne was smart, and she had things to say in defense of her religion.

In 1627, Anne's father moved the family to Boston, England, where Anne contracted the small pox but survived. She was now fifteen years old, and believed in her heart that God had saved her for a reason. She now began an inward journey to explore why this might be the case. This self-reflective behavior was unusual for a Puritan, let alone a fifteen-year-old girl.

When she was sixteen, Anne married Simon Bradstreet. He was ten years older than she, and he was now working for the Massachusetts Bay Company whose importance in the lives of the Dudley family and their Puritan friends would soon become apparent.

Violence in England under King Charles I was growing, especially against the Puritans who rejected the ideas of one King, one religion (Anglican), and one law (the King's). The King's wife was Catholic, and the Puritans felt the Anglican Church was far too Catholic as well. The Puritans were engaged in a struggle to practice what they felt was the true religion, but the violence against them was terrifying. Eventually, they believed their only choice for survival was to leave England. In 1629, Anne's father and husband set in motion a plan to leave for the New World—for America, with the backing of the Massachusetts Bay Company. They invited others to go with them. Anne's father was completely confident in the plan, but Anne was not. There were too many unknowns.

## America

On Easter Sunday, March 27, 1630, the Puritans set sail from Southampton with passengers, animals, and supplies. While Puritans did not always follow established Christian holidays, they felt this day was a good omen. But conditions onboard were dismal. These persons of minor nobility were not at all used to the stench from vomit and from people "relieving" themselves. Too many passengers were thrown together in small spaces. The food was barely edible, the sailors used offensive language, and it was cold. Spiritual and mental fortitude were essential for survival across the Atlantic. As Charlotte Gordon explains, "the hours alternated between terror and tedium."[3]

After seventy-seven days at sea, the *Arbella* fleet," as it was called (the lead ship was named for Lady Arbella, the wife of Sir Isaac Johnson, a founder of the Massachusetts Bay Company), did arrive safely and the Puritans viewed their successful voyage as a sign of God's approval. The leader of the colonists, John Winthrop, became governor of the new Massachusetts Bay Colony. Anne's father became Deputy Governor. Her husband became Chief Administrator. Originally, the colonists disembarked at Salem, Massachusetts, where an earlier group had established a settlement. But the villagers were sick, starving, nearly dead, and generally "bedraggled." Salem was no place to stay.[4]

The *Arbella* fleet continued south along the coast to Charlestown, where Anne saw Native Americans for the first time. Everything about Massachusetts was new and frightening to Anne—the sights, sounds, primitive conditions, and animals. Anne was miserable, and missed her fine home in England. No real house structures were built for months, so Anne's first home in the New World was quite uncomfortable. There was little food, physical hardship, and people from all stations in life were thrown together—some uneducated and irreligious. This was not at all what Anne was used to. And, it was winter in Massachusetts. Bone chilling.

To lift the colonists' spirits, John Winthrop and Thomas Dudley decided to form the first church in the new colony. They had left the Old World in part to start a reformed church. It was time, and Anne joined them in signing the covenant, which read:

*To unite ... into one Congregation, or Church, under the Lord Jesus Christ our Head ... and bind our selves to walke in all our wayses according to the Rule of the Gospell, and in all sincere Conformity to His holy ordinances, and in mutuall love, and respect each to other, so neere as God shall give us grace.*

But Charlestown was a disaster, and many colonists returned to England. Meanwhile, John Winthrop had found more fertile land and fresh water in what is now Boston (named after Boston, England). He, and many others, settled there. The Dudleys and Bradstreets opted for Newtowne, just across the Charles River from Boston, which was inland, safe, and on the river. Newtowne became the first seat of the colony's government. Anne and Simon built a house on Watchhouse Hill, near what is today Harvard Yard.

Anne was still childless. She believed she had fallen out of favor with God, and this was her punishment. Anne would never have considered the reason for her infertility to be caused by stress, hunger, and illness. Anne probably had one or more female servants to assist her, but she would have been integrally involved in preparing her household for another winter to avoid the disaster of the previous one. But Anne was very sick, and went to live with her parents instead. Charlotte Gordon points out that Anne believed her many illnesses were God's way of making her improve spiritually as she spent many hours alone in contemplation.[5]

## Poetry

Anne eventually recovered, and in 1632 she wrote her first poem in America—a tribute to God, titled "Upon a Fit of Sickness." As Gordon explains, "Whatever Anne's intentions on composing this first poem, it does seem clear that the act of writing offered her a way of coping with the hardships she had to tolerate. She transformed her loneliness, disappointment, and profound disillusionment into verse, drawing on what she had learned not only from her most recent illness but also from the voyage and the first year in America. In doing so she discovered the tool that would allow her to endure and make sense of her experience in the wilderness. Only through 'pain,' she declared, did she stand a chance to grow."[6]

Later in 1632, finding herself pregnant with her first child, Anne believed all of her prayers and thanks had been answered. Clearly, she believed, "poetry writing had ushered in a baby." But having children was a dangerous undertaking for women. Many died in childbirth. When Anne gave birth to a healthy boy, Samuel, in 1633, with only the help of women family and friends as there was

no midwife, Anne believed, "God allowed her to triumph."
The baby grew strong and thrived—further proof. Gordon
explains, "Motherhood was the most important way to
serve God. If she could help raise a new flock of the
faithful, Anne would help ensure the future of the New
England Puritan dream."[7]

In 1634, Anne's father became Governor of the
Massachusetts Bay Colony. Political conflict involving
a man named Roger Williams was dividing the colony.
Religious conflict in the person of Anne Hutchinson,
a spiritual guide and midwife, was similarly disruptive.
Anne's father wanted to leave what he viewed as the
corruption of Newtowne for a settlement on the frontier
—Ipswich—where he could shape another new town.
By now Anne had friends and neighbors she would have
to leave behind. She was pregnant again, and had a
two-year-old son to care for on the thirty-one-mile journey
North. It was always harder for women to simply pick up
and leave.

## Ipswich

Anne would be heading into another unknown
environment, but already approximately fifty people lived
in Ipswich—many of them people of means whom Anne
knew. Some were educated men with private libraries.
Ipswich would not be a desolate place intellectually, but it
was still "on the edge of the forest" and men carried guns
at all times.[8]

While the Bradstreets' house was being built, Anne
planted a housewife's garden to grow the herbs that
were essential for her to maintain her family's health and

keep her house clean. Anne's life was extremely busy, managing a new household, servants, and two small children. Her husband and father were often called away to Boston on business, leaving Anne alone. Charlotte Gordon writes, "It was poetry that enabled her to survive without falling into depression."[9]

Anne began to write late at night, when everyone else was asleep. It was the only time she had privacy in their small wooden house. She was entering into dangerous territory for a woman. Anne Hutchinson's inappropriate behavior in Boston was "proof" that women were too frail to engage in intellectual activity, or too crazy. Men, especially ministers, constantly debated how to limit female behavior and maintain the established (God ordained, they believed) patriarchal hierarchy. Anne could have become a target of anger if people knew she was writing. She would have been accused of abandoning her family, of vanity, and not accepting her rightful place. Anne's family did support her writing, but she kept it hidden from her neighbors.

Wisely and strategically, Anne decided to "write in the name of God" and to "pen righteous words" on behalf of the colony. How could people criticize? She also befriended Ipswich's minister, Nathaniel Ward, who initially railed against women who "got out of hand" but eventually came to admire Anne's intelligence. Nathaniel Ward let her use his extensive library, and they spent many hours together in conversation.[10]

His friendship must have brightened Anne's days when her parents moved to Boston in 1639, less than a year after her third child was born. At the same time, Simon was constantly traveling for his political work. Anne was now the single head of a frontier household, the "deputy husband" who handled all of the family's business and legal affairs. Anne's son, Simon, was born in 1640, and her daughter, Hannah, in 1642. Even so, she was deeply lonely.

## Voice

While Anne's early poems had been rather self-deprecating, they now struck a much bolder tone. She paid close attention to the political upheaval in England when King Charles dismissed Parliament and war broke out between supporters of Parliament and those of the King. In 1642, Anne wrote "A Dialogue between Old England and New England," describing an ailing mother (England) and her child (America). The "Old" needed to be purged of sin, while the "New" was righteous. This poem was dangerous for Anne to write, but no one else in the colony had offered a public opinion. As Charlotte Gordon writes, "[Anne] was not the miserably uncertain girl she had been back in England and on the *Arbella*. Instead, she was beginning to believe that she did indeed possess the God-given vocation to shout out the words of the New Jerusalem." Anne was now a social critic, speaking with a clear strong voice, and one that had a distinctly New England style.[11]

In 1646, Anne, Simon, and their large family moved to Andover (today, North Andover) where Simon once again wanted to help bring Puritanism to a frontier town. Anne's brother-in-law, John Woodbridge, served as the minister there. Anne was pregnant with her seventh child, and had to leave behind her beloved, learned friend Nathaniel Ward and his wonderful library. Who could she talk to now? As Charlotte Gordon explains, Andover was "an intellectual desert" for Anne. But she plunged into research on a poem about ancient civilizations ("The Four Elements") and women who stepped out of their prescribed roles, displayed unexpected courage, and achieved greatness.[12]

In John Woodbridge Anne did find another intellectual, but he was soon called to England to help resolve differences between King Charles and the Puritans. John took some of Anne's poems with him, as they were proof of God's grace in the New World. But would anyone believe Anne had written them? To make sure, Woodbridge brought testimonials written by prominent men with him.

Anne gave birth to her son Simon soon after arriving in Andover, and she was intensely lonely without her family or friends. Once again, she turned inward, to self-reflection and faith. Anne hadn't written a line for ten years, but when King Charles was beheaded in 1649 she took up her pen. No sitting monarch had ever been killed by his own people. Anne lamented this terrible course of events, and she sent the resulting poem to John Woodbridge in England for him to include in the book of her poems he was preparing.

On July 1, 1650, Anne's book, *The Tenth Muse, Lately Sprung Up in America*, appeared and it took the English public "by storm." Anne wrote that New England held the promise of peace. She was optimistic at a time when British people needed to hear such a hopeful message. The book was also a "curiosity" because she was a woman. Anne became a celebrity, and the voice of Puritan New England.[13]

Anne's eighth and last child, John, was born in 1652. By now, she had been pregnant, giving birth, or recovering from pregnancy for twenty years and she was exhausted. Anne's father died a short time later, followed by her former minister, John Cotton, who had emigrated to the colony in 1633. All of Anne's male teachers were now gone. Charlotte Gordon writes that Jesus now became the one man Anne could always count on. Her religiosity, her "passion for God," deepened. In fact, her intense loneliness gave her the opportunity to be closer to God.[14] As Anne's illnesses grew more frequent, she worried about her children and wrote a spiritual biography for them. In her poetry, she urged her Puritan readers to glory in God and the Massachusetts Bay Colony, God's chosen land. Eventually, she did grow strong again, and began editing *The Tenth Muse* for an American publication.

England's bloody civil war, headed by Oliver Cromwell, had finally ended and Parliament invited King Charles II to assume the throne. The new king stressed religious tolerance, and wondered whether or not the Massachusetts Bay Colony should continue. He urged the colonists to accept people of other faiths, but the Puritans dug in their heels. They banished Quakers, and other non-Puritans, and were determined to hang on to the "pure" church they had created. Anne wrote poetry defending the Puritan faith.

Anne now endured a series of tragedies. Her house caught on fire and was completely destroyed. She lost books, journals, and poems. Several precious grandchildren died, and she became more and more bereft. Her final poems focused on heaven, and how this world really was a "vale of sorrow." Finally, in 1672, at age fifty-nine, Anne Dudley Bradstreet died.

It is unknown where Anne's family buried her, but a memorial in her memory stands in the North Parish Burying Ground in North Andover. Several years after her death, in 1678, Anne's revised edition of *The Tenth Muse*, edited and with new poems added, was published in Boston as *Several Poems Compiled with Great Variety of Wit and Learning.*

## Her Faith in Action

If you've read this story, you can see what an active and guiding role God played in Anne's life. When she was ill and survived as a teenager, it was because God had spared her for a special purpose. While she was childless, she believed she had incurred God's displeasure. The opposite was true as she gave birth to more and more healthy children. For Puritans, success indicated God's approval. Failure demonstrated His disapproval.

As a Puritan, Anne was raised to feel "profoundly discouraged by her moral weakness," to know her flaws, and to strive for perfection. She knew her secret desires came from insecurity and vanity, and were sinful.[15]

But Puritan theology also encouraged the study of history as a testament to God's guiding hand. It stressed writing—for men. What's fascinating about Anne is how early she looked inward to deliberately examine her relationship with God. During so many bouts with loneliness and depression, she counted on her faith to sustain her. Those illnesses, however, were God's way of making her improve spiritually, she believed.

Anne believed with all of her being that Puritanism was the true faith, and she was poised to defend it with her life if necessary. At the end of the day, as Charlotte Gordon explains, each of her poems was an offering to God and to her community.[16]

## Sites to Visit in Massachusetts

Home of Anne Bradstreet's (site of)
33 High Street
Ipswich, MA 01938
*A bronze plaque marks the site of Anne's house. Further down High Street another plaque marks the site of her father's home.*

Anne Bradstreet Memorial
North Parish Burying Ground
190 Academy Road
North Andover, MA 01845
*It's possible Anne was buried here, but no one knows for certain.*

## Resources

*Mistress Bradstreet: The Untold Life of America's First Poet* by Charlotte Gordon (Little, Brown and Company, 2005)

Websites:
*Search for Anne Bradstreet at:*
Annebradstreet.com
Poetry Foundation

## Notes to the Biographical Sketch

1   *Mistress Bradstreet: The Untold Life of America's First Poet* by Charlotte Gordon (Little, Brown and Company, 2005), x.
2   Ibid., 13, 285.
3   Ibid., 101.
4   Ibid., 3.
5   Ibid.
6   Ibid., 130.
7   Ibid., 130, 136, 142.
8   Ibid., 173.
9   Ibid., 175.
10  Ibid., 179.
11  Ibid., 209, 210, 225.
12  Ibid., 230
13  Ibid., 249.
14  Ibid., 256.
15  Ibid.
16  Ibid., 128.

"If what I do prove well, it won't advance,
They'll say it's stolen, or else it was by chance."

———————————

"There is no object that we see; no action that we do; no good that we enjoy; no evil that we feel, or fear, but we may make some spiritual advantage of all: and he that makes such improvement is wise, as well as pious."

—*Anne Bradstreet*

"I am fully aware of the unpopularity of the task I have undertaken; but though I *expect* ridicule and censure, it is not in my nature to *fear* them.

A few years hence, the opinion of the world will be a matter in which I have not even the most transient interest; but this book will be abroad on its mission of humanity long after the hand that wrote it is mingling with the dust.

Should it be the means of advancing, even one single hour, the inevitable progress of truth and justice, I would not exchange the consciousness for all Rothchild's wealth of Sir Walter's fame."

—*Lydia Maria Francis Child,*
*from* An Appeal in Favor of That Class of Americans Called Africans*, 1833*

# Lydia Maria Francis Child

### (1802–1880)

---

## Her Achievements

- Prolific and successful novelist, editor, journalist and scholar
- Author of America's first anti-slavery book
- Author of the first historical novel in the United States
- Author of groundbreaking work on women in history
- Co-founder of the Boston Female Anti-Slavery Society and planner of anti-slavery fundraising fairs
- Early advocate for Native American rights
- Co-founder of Massachusetts Woman Suffrage Society

*(more)*

---

- Defender interracial marriage, divorce, and female sexuality
- One of the earliest women to earn a living through her writing

## Her Story

One of Lydia Maria Child's biographer's, Joan Goodwin, once wrote, "Lydia Maria Child was a novelist, editor, journalist and scholar who produced a body of work remarkable for its brilliance, originality and variety, much of it inspired by a strong sense of justice and love of freedom." Indeed, by the time Child passed away in 1880, having helped to bring about an end to slavery, she was one of the most successful, courageous, and prolific women writers in American history—and someone who risked income and fame to take the stands she did. As Carolyn Karcher wrote about her, "she boldly tackled problems of racial, sexual, and economic justice that our society has yet to resolve—problems she never allowed cynics to dismiss as insoluble."[1]

Born in Medford, Massachusetts, in 1802 to Susannah Rand Francis and Convers Francis, a successful baker and businessman, "Maria," as she later chose to be called (pronounced Mah-RY-ah), was heavily influenced by her older brother, also named Convers, who attended Harvard. Maria was allowed to read books from the library of the family's Congregational minister and developed a life-long love for literature, ideas, and education.

Sadly, in 1814, when Maria was twelve, her mother died of tuberculosis. At the time, Maria was enrolled in "Miss Swan's Academy" in Medford, but her father sent her to

Norridgewock, Maine, in 1815 to keep house for her newly married sister Mary. In Maine, Maria continued her studies and visited a Penobscot village to experience Native American ways first-hand.

Maria assumed her first teaching job at the age of eighteen in Gardiner, Maine, which had just become a free state through the Missouri Compromise (thus allowing Missouri to become a slave-holding state). In Maine, Maria discovered Swedenborgian theology, initiating a life-long fascination with, and tolerance for, world religions. Meanwhile, her brother, Convers, had become the minister of the (Unitarian) First Parish Church in Watertown, Massachusetts.

Returning to the Boston area in 1821, Maria was baptized in the (Congregational) First Parish Church in Medford, her childhood church. It was then that she chose the name "Maria" for herself. The following year, she became a member of the Boston Society of the New Jerusalem, or the Swedenborgian Society, whose members followed and practiced the teachings of Jesus.

## Writing

Maria published her first book in 1824, titled *Hobomok, A Tale of Early Times*. It was the first historical novel published in the United States, and it presented a strong defense of Native American rights. In her book, Maria told a love story between a colonial woman and a Native American man, presenting a controversial defense of interracial marriage. Although Maria had published *Hobomok* anonymously, readers discovered her real identity. The book sold well, and she became an instant celebrity and part of Boston's "literary scene." Maria followed *Hobomok* with two more historical novels: *Evenings in New England* and *The Rebels, or Boston Before the Revolution*. Both books sold well.

Now, Maria began to publish children's stories, and in 1826 she founded and became the editor of a children's magazine called the *Juvenile Miscellany*. That same year, she opened a school at the home in Watertown, Massachusetts, she shared with her brother Convers, welcoming the teenaged Margaret Fuller as one of her students. In Boston, she befriended Elizabeth Peabody and became part of the city's female intellectual elite.

In 1828, Maria married David Child, a Harvard graduate, lawyer, and publisher of the *Massachusetts Journal*. David had served briefly in the Massachusetts legislature, spoke at political rallies, and was active in the anti-slavery movement. Maria wrote for his newspaper, and learned to guard her earnings as her husband could be "impractical" with her money.[2]

The following year, 1829, Maria published America's first book of domestic advice geared toward lower income women—*The Frugal Housewife*. It was hugely popular, brought her substantial income, and served as a precursor to later books in this genre. Maria returned to her political writing that year with *The First Settlers*, a book that claimed that title for Native Americans, not Europeans. She presented a positive view of Native American religion, and strong female leaders within the tribal culture. By the end of 1829, the abolitionist William Lloyd Garrison was referring to Maria Child as the "First Woman in the Republic."

## Abolition

Maria Child finally met Garrison in 1830, and soon after began writing for his anti-slavery newspaper the *Liberator.* Financial difficulties forced her to take a teaching position while she continued to write and organize. In 1831, she co-founded the Boston Female Anti-Slavery Society with Maria Weston Chapman, the same year Nat Turner's Rebellion set pro-slavery whites on edge, and she became a leader within Garrison's New England Anti-Slavery Society in 1832.

That same year, Maria began to publish a series of biographical sketches of accomplished women in history. In fact, women's history was a theme she pursued throughout her literary life. Then, in 1833, with the publication of *An Appeal in Behalf of that Class of Americans Called Africans*, Maria Child became the first person in America to publish an anti-slavery book. In the book's introduction she wrote, "I am fully aware of the unpopularity of the task I have undertaken, but though I expect ridicule and censure, it is not in my nature to fear them."[3]

Maria Child paid a high price for her boldness. "Fans" of her children's magazine pulled their support and she had to shut it down. Her books stopped selling. The Boston Athenaeum suspended her library privileges. As Jone Johnson Lewis tells us, "Her popularity plummeted." Previously, it had been enviable. But, as Dorothy Emerson, one of her biographers explains, "Women who had battled for the cause of the slave and women who had fought for their own release from oppression found their voices and began to articulate their individuality. Whether consciously or not, they acted beyond women's sphere and entered the world of action and influence."[4]

During the latter part of the 1830s, Maria planned anti-slavery fundraising fairs, attended conventions, and continued to call for an immediate end to slavery. To further her work for women's rights, she published her biographical sketches of women as a book titled *History of the Condition of Women*. This work was followed by *Authentic Anecdotes of American Slavery*.

In 1835, Maria attended the anti-slavery convention in Philadelphia where she met the Quaker abolitionist Angelina Grimké. The following year, she published *Anti-Slavery Catechism* and *The Evils of Slavery, and the Cure of Slavery*. For Maria Child, along with her activist colleagues including Maria Weston Chapman, Mary Livermore, and Lucy Stone, their work was about justice and equality for everyone—women, African Americans, and Native Americans. For them, it was all connected.

In 1837, Maria attempted to restore her "family friendly" voice by publishing *The Family Nurse*, but the book was unsuccessful. Meanwhile, she continued to attend anti-slavery conventions and was elected to the executive committee of William Lloyd Garrison's American Anti-Slavery Society (AASS).

Between 1841 and 1843, Maria moved to New York to serve as the editor of the *National Anti-Slavery Standard*, the AASS's weekly newspaper. She needed the money, after another one of her husband's failed enterprises. Eventually, in 1843, she was able to separate her finances from David's, and after an editorial disagreement with

Garrison she left to write *Letters from New York* about her experiences. Luckily, this book was quite popular and Maria regained some of the fame and admiration she had lost earlier because of her political stands. In 1844, she returned to writing for children and published the work she is best known for: "Over the River and Through the Woods."

With the passage of the Fugitive Slave Law in 1850, under which Northerners were legally bound to return escaped slaves to the South, Maria kept up her anti-slavery writing. She wrote pieces for the progressive *New-York Tribune* when the abolitionist Senator Charles Sumner was nearly caned to death by a Southern colleague on the Senate floor, and when "civil war" raged in Kansas over the issue of allowing slavery. In 1859, as John Brown sat in prison after his raid on Harper's Ferry, Maria wrote to him and offered to nurse him back to health. She sent copies of these letters to the Governor of Virginia who published them in a local newspaper. Later, Maria's letters were published as a pamphlet and widely distributed. After John Brown's hanging, Maria helped to plan a service for him in Boston at Tremont Temple.

## War

In 1861, with the outbreak of the Civil War, Maria Child edited Harriet Jacobs' autobiography, *Incidents in the Life of a Slave-Girl*, and made sure it was published. Harriet Jacobs' book caused a sensation. More of Maria's anti-slavery tracts followed, and by 1864, the year after President Lincoln issued The Emancipation Proclamation, she joined others in calls for education and the redistribution of land for African Americans in the South. That same year, Maria met the sculptor Edmonia Lewis at an anti-slavery reception in Boston. In 1865, Maria wrote *The Freedmen's Book*, a reading primer for former slaves that included writings by African Americans, and she mourned the assassination of President Lincoln.

## Tolerance

Maria kept on writing, about world religions and tolerance, about Native Americans, and about growing old gracefully. Sadly, her brother, Convers, had passed away in 1863, and her husband died in 1874. She became involved with the Massachusetts Woman Suffrage Association, and the Free Religious Association founded by a group of Unitarians in Boston. She published *Aspirations of the World* about world religions, pledging "to do all I can to enlarge and strengthen the hand of human brotherhood." Maria Child had been a woman of faith and theological inquiry throughout her life as a Congregationalist, Swedenborgian, and Unitarian.

As the Rev. Dorothy Emerson wrote about her, there was a "constant crossing of boundaries between religion and social action"—an example of 'lived religion' that acted and didn't wait for things to change." In 1879, when William Lloyd Garrison died, a leading figure in Maria's social action work, she published a tribute to him in *The Atlantic Magazine*.[5]

The following year, 1880, Lydia Maria Child died in Wayland, Massachusetts, where she had moved in 1853 to care for her ailing father She was buried there next to her husband. Maria died childless, despite the dozens of articles, books, and magazines for children she had generated. Her publications on abolition, women's rights, and Native American rights numbered in the dozens. In her eulogy, the abolitionist Wendell Phillips noted that she was "ready to die for a principle and starve for an idea ... We felt that neither fame, nor gain, nor danger, nor calumny had any weight with her."[6]

## Her Faith in Action

As Joan Goodwin wrote about Maria Child, she was "engaged in a religious search that would continue her whole life." Raised in the Medford, Massachusetts, Congregational church, Maria was exposed early on to the minister's library. She read about world religions, and while at the time she embraced traditional Christianity and, as a young woman, adopted Swedenborgianism, she nonetheless "wanted a faith that was free from dogma, and would embrace world religions ... She was lonely religiously, dissatisfied with the institutional church and hungry for spiritual nourishment," Joan Goodwin writes. Maria not only read about non-Christian religions, she visited a Native American village in Maine to learn and write about their spiritual lives.[8]

Maria herself once wrote:

"I am more in danger of wrecking on the rocks of skepticism than of standing on the shoals of fanaticism. I am apt to regard a system of religion as I do any other beautiful theory. It plays round the imagination, but fails to reach the heart. I wish I could find some religion in which my heart and understanding could unite; that amidst the darkest clouds of this life I might ever be cheered with the mild halo of religious consolation."

Maria's authorship of a book on world religions, one of the earliest in America, and her membership in the Free Religious Association speak volumes about her commitment to religious tolerance and respectful inquiry. To repeat her words, she pledged "to do all I can to enlarge and strengthen the hand of human brotherhood." In Boston, Maria was a follower of the Unitarian minister William Ellery Channing who taught her, "To be truly virtuous, all that was needed was a rejuvenated conscience and a commitment to a life of Christian benevolence,"

Dorothy Emerson explains. "Church, government, and other external controls would vanish in the millennium. Such views accorded perfectly with Maria's own. Impatient with sectarian constraints and impelled by a fierce love of freedom, she shared this radical vision. She longed to rid the world of tyranny and oppression; and what better way than by abolishing slavery?"[9]

And here's where Maria's faith moved into action.

One of Maria Child's colleagues in the anti-slavery movement, Maria Weston Chapman, explained the connection between their political work and religion this way: "The Holy Spirit did actually descend upon men and women in tongues of flame … All suppression of selfishness makes the moments great; and mortals were never more sublimely forgetful of self than were the abolitionists in those early days, before the mortal force which emanated from them had become available as a political power. Ah, my friend, that is the only true church organization, when heads and hearts unite in working for the welfare of the human race."[10]

To repeat Dorothy Emerson's observation, Maria Child's life exemplified a "constant crossing of boundaries between religion and social action" providing "an example of 'lived religion' that acted and didn't wait for things to change."[11]

## Sites to Visit in Massachusetts

Home of Lydia Maria Child
270 Main Street
Watertown, MA 02472
*Maria lived here with her brother, Convers, a Unitarian minister, before she married. Here, she tutored the teenaged Margaret Fuller, and developed a lifelong friendship with her.*

Home of Lydia Maria Child (site of)
Joy's Building, 81 Washington Street
Boston, MA 02108
*Maria lived at this site after her marriage to David Child.*

Home of Lydia Maria Child
Old Sudbury Road
Wayland, MA 01778
*Maria moved to Wayland, to her father's house, in 1853.*

Grave Site of Lydia Maria Child
North Cemetery
Wayland, MA 01778

Elizabeth Peabody's Bookstore and Home
15 West Street
Boston, MA 02108
*Maria Child attended the "Conversations" for women held here by Margaret Fuller and was part of the Boston female intellectual elite who participated.*

The Boston Athenaeum
10 1/2 Beacon Street
Boston, MA 02108
*The Athenaeum was located on Pearl Street in Maria's time. The Athenaeum revoked Maria's library privileges after she published her first anti-slavery book.*

Federal Street Church (site of)
Corner of Franklin and Federal Streets
Boston, MA 02108
*Maria attended this church led by Rev. William Ellery Channing. Today, a plaque marks the spot.*

## Resources

*Crusader for Freedom: A Life of Lydia Maria Child* by Deborah Pickman Clifford (Beacon Press, 1992).

*Standing Before Us: Unitarian Universalist Women and Social Reform, 1776—1936* by Dorothy May Emerson (Skinner House Books, 2000).

*The First Woman of the Republic: A Cultural Biography of Lydia Maria Child* by Carolyn L. Karcher (Duke University Press, 1994).

*American Women's History: An A to Z of People, Organizations, Issues, and Events* by Doris Weatherford (Prentice Hall, 1994).

Websites:
*Search for Lydia Maria Child at:*
About.com
Dictionary of Unitarian Universalist Biography
National Women's History Museum

## Notes to the Biographical Sketch

1 Lydia Maria Child" by Joan Goodwin, in *Dictionary of Unitarian Universalist Biography* (online), and *The First Woman of the Republic: A Cultural Biography of Lydia Maria Child* by Carolyn L. Karcher (Duke University Press, 1994), xii.
2 Goodwin.
3 *An Appeal in Behalf of that Class of Americans Called Africans* by Lydia Maria Child (Allen and Ticknor, 1833), introduction.
4 "Lydia Maria Child" by Jone Johnson Lewis in *About.com* (online), and *Standing Before Us: Unitarian Universalist Women and Social Reform, 1776—1936* by Dorothy May Emerson (Skinner House Books, 2000), 285.
5 Emerson, 282.
6 Goodwin.
7 Goodwin.
8 Goodwin.
9 Emerson, 280.
10 Emerson, 281.
11 Emerson, 282.

"If you ask me what office women may fill;
I will reply—any. I do not care what case
you put; let them be sea-captains if you will
... We would have every arbitrary barrier
thrown down. We would have every path laid
open to woman as freely as to man ... Can
we wonder that many reformers think that
measures are not likely to be taken in behalf
of women, unless their wishes could be
publicly represented by women?"

———————

"The Power who gave a power, signifies that
the intellect must be brought out towards
perfection."

—*Margaret Fuller*

# Margaret Fuller

## (1810–1850)

### Her Achievements

- First American to write a book about equality for women
- First woman foreign correspondent and first woman war correspondent to serve under combat conditions
- First woman journalist for Horace Greeley's *New-York Tribune*, and first woman literary editor of a major American newspaper
- First editor of the *Dial*, the Transcendentalist journal, making her the first woman in America to edit an intellectual publication

*(more)*

- First woman literary critic who also set literary standards for American writers
- First woman to enter the Harvard College library to pursue research

## Her Story

In her memoirs, Margaret Fuller recalled, "I remember how, a little child, I had stopped myself one day on the stairs, and asked, how came I here? How is it that I seem to be this Margaret Fuller? What does it mean? What shall I do about it?" Many years later, when she led her "Conversations" for women in Boston to explore philosophical, theological, and political questions, she asked them to think about what for her were two centrally guiding questions: "What were we born to do, and how shall we do it?"[1]

Imagine growing up in a world, in the 1810s, when the message for girls was, "Who you are really doesn't matter. Getting married and raising children are your sole purpose. You exist to serve others and nothing more." Luckily, Margaret Fuller was able to push beyond these barriers.

## Foundations

Sarah Margaret Fuller, born on May 23, 1810 in Cambridge, Massachusetts, was the oldest child of Timothy Fuller, a Harvard-educated attorney, and Margarett Crane Fuller. With the death of an infant sister, young Margaret was an only child for several years and the center of her father's attention in particular. Timothy Fuller planned a rigorous course of study for his daughter.

"To excel in all things should be your constant aim," he told her. "Mediocrity is obscurity."[2]

By the time Margaret was 3 1/2 years old, Timothy was teaching her how to read and write; at 4 1/2, he taught her arithmetic; just before the age of five, she learned English and Latin grammar. Even when Timothy Fuller was elected to Congress and spent many months in Washington, D.C., he directed Margaret's studies by mail. Margaret also read voraciously: political philosophy, great European authors and playwrights, ancient and recent history, travel, biography, and even novels—much to her father's consternation.

When Timothy Fuller was at home, father and daughter conversed in the evenings about what she was learning. "In the process," biographer Joan von Mehren explains, "Margaret developed a well-stored mind, a remarkable facility with the spoken word and foreign languages, and the exhilarating sense that she was very alive under tension." Margaret's father stressed analytical skills, logic, and "the correct use of language," according to von Mehren. Timothy Fuller's goal was to have his daughter develop "a secure and favored place in an ordered republican society" that was consistent with his Enlightenment values.[3]

At age nine, Margaret attended the Cambridge Port Private Grammar School ("The Port School") whose master was a Harvard graduate. By age ten, she had command of the standard classics in translation and was beginning to learn French. She was known as the "smart one," according to classmate Oliver Wendell Holmes. The following year, Margaret attended Dr. Park's Boston

Lyceum for Young Ladies where she was ridiculed for her "country ways." She was now studying Italian, French, and geography, and attending dancing school.[4]

Fearing their daughter's potential "unmarriageability," the Fullers sent Margaret for a brief time to Susan Prescott's more traditional Young Ladies' Seminary in rural Groton, Massachusetts. But she soon returned to The Port School to study Greek and Latin. Eventually, at the age of fifteen and with her father's assistance, Margaret Fuller created her own course of self-study, which included lessons with the author Lydia Maria Francis (later, Child).

At the same time, Margaret became friends with a group of young Harvard students who were caught up in a heady time of intellectual, literary, and theological activity at the college. German philosophy, literature, and poetry were the "craze," and many of these young men (James Freeman Clarke, Frederic Henry Hedge, William Henry Channing) were preparing for leadership roles in the Unitarian church. Margaret borrowed books from them, and invited the men home for lively exchanges of ideas.

Like her Harvard friends, Margaret discovered the German philosopher and literary giant Johann Wolfgang von Goethe, who was regarded as a leading thinker by American Transcendentalists. In 1833, when the Fuller family moved to a farm in Groton, Massachusetts, Margaret felt terribly isolated from Cambridge and Boston, but she viewed her time there as her "graduate school" and began to study German in earnest.[5]

## Teaching

Margaret Fuller's teaching career really began at home, where she was responsible for the early education of her younger siblings. But it was in Groton that she began earning money for the first time by adding neighborhood children to her home-based classroom. While in Groton, Fuller also began writing for publications. Her first article of literary criticism (an emerging field in America), appeared in 1834 in her friend George Bancroft's *Boston Daily Advertiser*. She then wrote literary and dramatic criticism, and translated Goethe for her friend James Freeman Clarke's *Western Messenger*.

Fuller now began to understand that teaching young people and publishing articles were part of her larger role in life as a public educator. As Joan von Mehren explains, "Teaching was natural to her, and she would, in fact, never cease being a teacher in one guise or another."[6]

In 1835, when her father died suddenly, Margaret wrote to her brother Richard, "Nothing sustains me now but the thought that God ... must have some good for me to do." She was considered the de facto head of her family now, and their finances were meager. Margaret needed paid work, and an opportunity surfaced the following year in Concord, Massachusetts. There, during her first visit to Ralph Waldo Emerson's home, she met Bronson Alcott whose innovative Temple School in Boston would soon be without a teacher due to Elizabeth Peabody's resignation.[7]

While Margaret waited for Alcott's job offer, she decided to move to Boston to start language and literature classes for women in German, Italian, and French. Before she left Concord, Emerson "kindly" identified "lapses" in her education. He steered Fuller toward the German and British philosophers and writers she would have studied if she had been able to attend college.[8]

Margaret's time at the Temple School was short due to Alcott's controversial methods and the eventual closing of his school but, while there, she taught Latin, French, Italian, and kept records of the students' "conversation classes" in which they were encouraged to really explore subjects intellectually and engage in intelligent dialog.

In 1837, once again in need of work, Margaret accepted a well-paid position at Hiram Fuller's Greene Street School in Providence, Rhode Island, where she was put in charge of sixty students. There, she taught Latin, composition, elocution, history, natural philosophy, ethics, and the New Testament of the Bible. Margaret 's students described her as "strict and demanding, witty and authoritarian, at times unreasonable but always formidable, challenging, and impressive." In fact, students were drawn to the school because of Margaret 's reputation.

In the evenings, Margaret taught German language classes for women and men and worked on a biography of Goethe. She joined the intellectual Coliseum Club where she delivered her first public speech on "the sorry relation of women to society." Earlier, during a visit to Concord, Margaret participated in gatherings of the "Transcendentalist Club"—the first time women were allowed as members in a "major male intellectual society," according to biographer Charles Capper. Before leaving Providence due to her failing health, Fuller observed, "I am not without my dreams and hopes as to the education of women."[9]

Returning to Boston, Margaret made plans to hold what she called "Conversations" for women at Elizabeth Peabody's bookstore on West Street. Her initial purpose was not at all political. Instead, Margaret was interested in exploring what were to her THE two fundamental questions: "What were we born to do? How shall we do it?"

These were questions "which so few ever propose to themselves 'til their best years are gone by," Fuller explained. At the very least, she hoped to provide "a point of union to well-educated and thinking women" where they could satisfy their "wish for some such means of stimulus and cheer, and ... for a place where they could state their doubts and difficulties with hope of gaining aid from the experience or aspirations of others."[10]

Margaret's lucrative Conversations continued for five years and attracted approximately 200 students. Among them were some of the most prominent women intellects, authors, and reformers in New England including Julia Ward Howe, Lydia Maria Child, Ednah Dow Cheney, and Lidian Emerson. Eventually, given the heightened political activity in Boston on the subjects of slavery and women's rights, Margaret's Conversations took a decidedly political turn.

## Voice

In 1840, when Margaret Fuller agreed to serve as the first editor of the *Dial* at Ralph Waldo Emerson's request, she propelled herself even further into the public eye.

While Margaret shunned the "Transcendentalist" label for herself, the *Dial* provided a vehicle for Transcendentalists to explain and defend themselves from criticism and misinterpretation. The *Dial* served as a forum for new authors and new ideas. Margaret saw the publication as "a perfectly free organ ... for the expression of individual thought and character, [one that would] not aim at leading public opinion, but at stimulating each man to think for himself."[11]

Margaret solicited work from such writers (and friends) as Bronson Alcott, Frederic Henry Hedge, Caroline Sturgis, Ellery Channing, Henry David Thoreau, Theodore Parker, Elizabeth Peabody, George and Sophia Ripley, and, of course, Emerson. She also provided her own articles on literary and cultural criticism and biography. Fuller's 1841 article on Goethe brought her acclaim as a leader in American cultural thought, and perhaps prompted her first visit to Brook Farm, the Utopian Transcendentalist community in West Roxbury, Massachusetts, founded by the Ripleys.

One of the key areas where Transcendentalists and other reformers clashed was on the subject of social and political change. Should reform happen within the individual or by tackling institutions and taking radical action? At the time, Fuller shied away from joining any particular group, preferring to examine many sides. But her two-year stint as editor of the *Dial* set her on a path toward radicalism and shaping public opinion.

Due to the financial instability of the publication Fuller never received her promised payment for being editor, so in 1842 she resigned. Emerson told her, "You have played martyr a little too long alone: let there be rotation in martyrdom!" and she gratefully turned over the editorship of the *Dial* to him. Margaret spent time that summer traveling with generous friends in New England who paid her expenses. In Boston, she continued her language classes and Conversations, which became increasingly political.

## Equality

In an 1843 edition of the *Dial*, Emerson published the essay that would initiate the next phase of Fuller's public life. In "The Great Lawsuit: Man vs. Men and Woman vs. Women," she held up the egalitarian ideals of the American Revolution. Fuller pointed out that while these ideals did not yet apply to women, African Americans, and Native Americans, Americans had a "special mission" to strive toward a just social system—and to assist others in the world who were initiating their own revolutions. Human freedom was a right, she asserted.

Fuller also threw out the ideology of "separate spheres" for women and men, instead addressing the conflicts between what was "male" and what was "female" within each person. She looked at gender roles in male and female friendships, and the laws and customs associated with marriage (subjects she also examined in her personal life as a single woman with male friends and married friends). She boldly exposed patriarchy and its effects. Fuller's groundbreaking essay caught the attention of another outspoken literary reformer—Horace Greeley, the publisher of the progressive *New-York Tribune*. He printed an excerpt of "The Great Lawsuit" in his newspaper in 1843, later, as a book: *Woman in the Nineteenth Century.*

Meanwhile, Fuller traveled to what was then considered the "western frontier" (Illinois and Wisconsin) with James Freeman Clarke, his sister, Sarah, an artist, and their mother, Rebecca, where she wanted to experience the American wilderness for herself. She hoped to find instances of socially progressive communities far away from the more rigid East. Instead, what caught her attention were the consequences of the displacement of Native peoples and the struggles of the settlers, especially the women, to survive difficult conditions.

Margaret saw the disparity between the promise of America and the reality of America, and the result was her 1844 book *Summer on the Lakes, in 1843*—an honest, first-hand account of conditions out west and a condemnation of U.S. policy. Biographer Charles Capper explains that she "[put] the region on the national literary and intellectual map and attract[ed] a national audience."[12]

*Summer on the Lakes* was the first time Fuller used her own name in her work; the research she completed at Harvard made her the first woman to use Harvard's library. According to Capper, Thomas Wentworth Higginson remembered seeing her "sitting, day after day, under the covert gaze of undergraduates who had never before looked upon a woman reading within those sacred precincts." Once again, Margaret's boldness caught the attention of Horace Greeley. He offered her a job in New York.[13]

## Fame

Horace Greeley put Margaret Fuller's essays on Page One of his reform-minded newspaper, the *New-York*

*Tribune.* She signed them with the symbol of a star, or an asterisk. Greeley paid Margaret the same salary as a man's, gave her a place to live when she first arrived, and encouraged her to write with "force." Margaret thus became the first woman in America to head the literary department of a major newspaper.

Margaret reviewed books (American and foreign), periodicals, musical events, concerts, lectures, and art exhibits. She visited and wrote about New York's "benevolent" institutions—prisons, hospitals, almshouses, insane asylums, homes for the blind and deaf. Now in a position to influence popular culture and social policy through first-hand observations, her urge to tell the truth and exceptional writing talent brought her fully into the public arena. Greeley saw her as "a philanthropist, preeminently a critic, a relentless destroyer of shams and outward traditions."[14]

Margaret's social commentary included condemnations of the approaching war with Mexico, the annexation of Texas, and the expansion of slavery. As historians Judith Mattson Bean and Joel Myerson explain, "She realizes that a war would drastically reconfigure the nation's population and landscape, leaving a legacy of dispossession and ethnic conflict. Fuller's essays actively resist American imperialism with attempts to subvert racist American expansionist rhetoric ... [her] participation in this debate was significant for another reason: the war with Mexico played a critical role in her disillusionment with America ... she began to equate U.S. national policy with European despotism and imperialism."[15]

America's national identity was in crisis in the 1840s. There were questions about American literary independence from Europe and the United States' responsibility to foreign revolutionaries. Bean and Myerson point out: "In reviewing contemporary American literature, Fuller practices a democratic criticism that challenges writers to uphold ideals of liberty and equality. Her political essays also argue that America's principles of liberty and equality are endangered by American materialism, greed, and the desire for continental domination. She directs attention to the relation of dominant American society to the other, contending that American society is founded upon tolerance and upon recognition of universal human rights rather than domination by force."[16]

In 1846, learning that her friends Marcus and Rebecca Spring would be traveling to Europe to observe new and effective social institutions, Margaret and Horace Greeley decided she should go as well and send dispatches to the *Tribune* from the cities, towns, and countries she visited. Before she left New York, Margaret wrote to her brother Richard, "I have now a position when if I can devot[e] myself entirely to use its occasions, a noble career is yet before me ... I want that my friends should wish me now to act in my public career."[17]

**Reformer**

In Europe, where industrialization was more advanced than in the United States, Margaret hoped to find successful models of communities and institutions to prevent the expansion of poverty back home. During this time of steamships, railroads, telegraphs, and booming emigration to American cities, Bean and Myerson explain,

"She envisions American culture as receiving not only people but seeds of thought and expression from other nations." These "thoughts" could be cultural as well as social and political.[18]

In Liverpool and Manchester, England, Margaret went to Mechanics Institutes where anyone (male or female) with five shillings could attend lectures, take courses, or see art exhibitions. In London, she reported on cultural and literary goings-on. In Paris, when she visited homes, hospitals, and day care centers for the sick children of the poor, she observed evening schools where boys were taught a trade. In her dispatches to the Tribune, she recommended that America immediately adopt such measures.

But it was the urban poverty of the slums that affected Margaret most of all, and the clear need for reform. In a dispatch from France she wrote, "The need of some radical measures of reform is not less strongly felt in France than elsewhere, and the time will come before long when such will be imperatively demanded." She also wrote, "To themselves be woe, who have eyes and see not, ears and hear not, the convulsions and sobs of injured Humanity."[19]

Two questions plagued Margaret's mind: What was her role in what she was witnessing? What was America's role?

As Joan von Mehren points out, after visiting Paris, "Every one of her columns now made some plea on behalf of its 'injured Humanity.'" While the initial purpose of Fuller's journey to Europe was "to seek useful ideas to transplant to the new world," she was transformed by her experience into "a radical vocation to communicate the monstrous suffering and human waste of the historical movement."[20]

If there was any doubt in Margaret's mind about her stature as an international voice, there was no doubt in the minds of her new European friends. Her reputation preceded her. They seemed to know she was destined to bridge the two continents and promote the reforms that were in their mutual interest. They embraced her.

In England, she renewed her acquaintance with social commentator Harriet Martineau, met the poet William Wordsworth, and the co-editors of the *People's Journal* Mary and William Howitt, whose modern marriage she had described in *Woman in the Nineteenth Century*. She also met Giuseppe Mazzini, the legendary exiled Italian revolutionary about whom Margaret had written for the *Tribune*. She was drawn to his cause and became his confidante and secret messenger.

In Paris, Margaret met George Sand and Pierre Leroux, who invited her to publish work in their periodical *La Revue Indépendante*. She was introduced to the exiled Polish revolutionary and poet Adam Mickiewicz, who became a kind of spiritual guide. Fuller was in her element, filled with a sense of purpose and armed with the skills and mechanism (the Tribune) to make a difference. But the best was yet to come—Italy.

### Revolutionary

Margaret Fuller arrived in Italy in March 1847, carrying secret letters from Mazzini and knowing she was heading into a turbulent political situation. What Mazzini and his supporters hoped to forge was a united Italian Republic starting with Rome, where the new Pope, Pius IX, seemed open to reform. The revolutionaries wanted to limit the Pope's power to spiritual matters; secular matters, like governance, should be left to democratically elected officials. With Rome as the head of a new republic, the rest of the independent states comprising Italy could join and form one democratic nation. Austrian and French forces, in particular, had other ideas. So did the Pope, whom Margaret took on in one of her more gutsy dispatches to the *Tribune*.

Among Mazzini's supporters was the Marchese Giovanni Angelo Ossoli, the youngest son of an aristocratic Catholic family with ties to the Pope. Margaret fell in love with him, and gave birth to their child, Angelo Eugene Phillip Ossoli ("Nino") in 1848 in Rieti where she had temporarily relocated for their safety. She returned to Rome as soon as she found caretakers for Nino, and resumed her work as the first woman foreign correspondent for a major newspaper to serve in wartime.

Margaret observed the Roman Revolution first-hand, managed a hospital, assisted her husband on the front lines, and began to write a modern history of the movement. In one of her last dispatches from Rome she wrote, "The New Era is no longer an embryo; it is born; it begins to walk—this very year sees its first giant steps, and can no longer mistake its features. Men have long been talking of a transition state—it is over—the power of positive, determinate efforts is begun." However, Margaret did not believe republican forms of government would take hold in Europe until the next century, and she was right.[21]

The Ossolis (Margaret began to refer to herself as the Countess Ossoli and assured her friends that she was married) escaped from Rome in 1850 as the revolution fell apart. Although she had a nightmare about the voyage and wrote to friends that she had a terrible sense of foreboding, the family eventually sailed for New York where Margaret knew she could find a publisher for her history of the revolution.

It was a dismal journey. The captain died of cholera on the way which Nino, Margaret's baby, also contracted. Before the steamer *Elizabeth* could reach its destination, and under the direction of a less experienced captain, a storm crossed its path, the ship ran aground, and eventually capsized just off Fire Island, New York. Some passengers were rescued, while others waited for help. Onlookers looted the items that washed ashore.

All three Ossolis perished at sea, along with Margaret's manuscript of the Roman Revolution. Only Nino's body was recovered, and he was buried in the Fuller family plot at Mount Auburn Cemetery in Cambridge, Massachusetts, where a cenotaph in Margaret Fuller Ossoli's memory now stands.

In a plea to her American audience from Rome, Margaret had written, "I pray you do something; let [the revolution] not end in a mere cry of sentiment … Do you owe no tithe to heaven for the privileges it has showered on you, for whose achievements so many here suffer and perish daily? Deserve to retain them by helping your fellow-men to acquire them … Friends, countrymen, and lovers of

virtue, lovers of freedom, lovers of truth!—be on the alert;
rest not supine in your easier lives, but remember

'Mankind is one
And beats with one great heart'"[22]

## Her Faith in Action

Margaret Fuller was raised in the Cambridgeport Unitarian
church. Her family tradition included "devotions of prayers
and hymn singing and faithfully attending the Sunday
meetings at church," according to her biographer Charles
Capper. But Christianity was not of particular interest
to Margaret or her father, who heavily influenced her
education, although she would revisit the subject later in
life. As a girl, Margaret read Greek and Roman mythology,
which taught her that other, legitimate religions existed.

Recalling her childhood, she wrote in her memoirs:

"I remember how, a little child, I had stopped myself one
day on the stairs, and asked, how came I here? How is
it that I seem to be this Margaret Fuller? What does it
mean? What shall I do about it?

I saw how long it must be before the soul can learn to act
under these limitations of time and space, and human
nature; but I saw, also, that it MUST do it—that it must
make all this false true—and sow new and immortal plants
in the garden of God, before it could return again.

I saw there was no self; that selfishness was all folly,
and the result of circumstance; that it was only because
I thought self real that I suffered; that I had only to live

in the idea of the ALL, and all was mine. This truth came to me, and I received it unhesitatingly; so that I was for that hour taken up into God. In that true ray most of the relations of earth seemed mere films, phenomena.

My earthly pain at not being recognized never went deep after this hour. I had passed the extreme of passionate sorrow; and all check, all failure, all ignorance have seemed temporary ever since … Since then I have suffered, as I must suffer again, till all the complex be made simple, but I have never been in discord with the grand harmony."[24]

As a teenager, Margaret befriended a group of young men at Harvard who were studying Goethe, the German philosopher who so influenced the American Transcendentalists. While Margaret didn't describe herself as a Transcendentalist, she became very involved in the self-reflective, life purpose issues that engaged people like Ralph Waldo Emerson and James Freeman Clarke, and so many others in Cambridge, Boston, and Concord. She believed in the Transcendentalist statement that "the Power who gave a power, signifies that the intellect must be brought out towards perfection."[25]

Perhaps the most telling moment for her spiritually was when she wrote to her brother after their father's death. His passing devastated her; he had been the centrally important person in her life, and she was uncertain if she could—or wanted to—go on without him. But, she wrote to her brother, "Nothing sustains me now but the thought that God … must have some good for me to do."[26]

And since her father's death, she "did" relentlessly—she taught, wrote, published, and became the "first" in so many areas for women. It's clear that she understood the mutual relationship she had with God. God had given her gifts it was her duty to use to help others. Margaret transformed the lives of Western women, and propelled the women's rights movement in the United States.

We can only hope that as the ship she sailed home on sank, that she was able to say to herself, "I figured out my life purpose, and I did it."

**Sites to Visit in Massachusetts**
(For a more complete list of sites, please visit the "history trails" section in historysmiths.com's store. There you will find a brochure titled "Margaret Fuller's Footsteps in New England.")

Birthplace of Margaret Fuller (Margaret Fuller House)
71 Cherry Street
Cambridge, MA 02139
*Margaret was born here on May 23, 1810.*

Home of Margaret Fuller (site of)
Corner of Ellery and Dana Streets
Cambridge, MA 02138
*The Fullers lived in the "Dana Mansion" on this site from 1826 to 1832.*

Home of Margaret Fuller
8 Ellery Street
Cambridge, MA 02139
*Margaret lived here from 1842 to 1844, writing* Summer on the Lakes, in 1843 *in this house.*

Harvard College Library
Harvard University Campus
Cambridge, MA 02138
*In 1843, while conducting research for her book* Summer
on the Lakes, in 1843, *Margaret became the first woman
to use Harvard's library.*

Margaret Fuller Cenotaph
Mount Auburn Cemetery
580 Mount Auburn Street
Cambridge, MA 02138
*Margaret's body was never recovered from the shipwreck,
but her family erected a cenotaph in her memory.*

Temple School (site of)
Masonic Temple
Corner of Tremont Street and Temple Place
Boston, MA 02111
*Margaret taught school here starting in 1836.*

Elizabeth Peabody's Bookstore
15 West Street
Boston, MA 02111
*Margaret held her "Conversations" for women here from
1839 to 1844.*

Federal Street Church (site of)
Corner of Franklin and Federal Streets
Boston, MA 02111
*Like many of her Transcendentalist friends, Margaret
attended this church led by William Ellery Channing.*

Home of Ralph Waldo Emerson
28 Cambridge Turnpike
Concord, MA 01742
*Margaret was a frequent guest in this house.*

Home of Margaret Fuller
"The Elms"
108 Pleasant Street/"Farmer's Row"
Groton, MA 01450
*The Fuller family lived here from 1833 to 1855.*

Greene Street School (site of)
Washington and Green Streets
Providence, RI 02903
*Margaret taught school here starting in 1837.*

## Resources

*Margaret Fuller, Critic: Writings from the New-York Tribune, 1844-1846* by Judith Mattson Bean and Joel Myerson (Columbia University Press, 2000).

*Minerva and the Muse* by Joan von Mehren (UMass Press, 1994).

*Margaret Fuller: An American Romantic Life, The Private Years* by Charles Capper (Oxford University Press, 1992).
*Margaret Fuller: An American Romantic Life, The Public Years* by Charles Capper (Oxford University Press, 2007).

Websites
*Search for Margaret Fuller at:*
Dictionary of Unitarian Universalist Biography
MargaretFuller.org

## Notes to the Biographical Sketch

1   *The Memoirs of Margaret Fuller Ossoli* by Margaret Fuller (University of Michigan Library, 2005).
2   *Margaret Fuller: An American Romantic Life, The Private Years* by Charles Capper (Oxford University Press, 1992).
3   *Minerva and the Muse* by Joan von Mehren (UMass Press, 1994).
4   Capper, *The Private Years.*
5   Ibid.
6   Von Mehren.
7   Ibid.
8   Ibid.
9   Capper, *The Private Years.*
10   Von Mehren.
11   Ibid.
12   Capper, *The Public Year*s.
13   Ibid.
14   Ibid.
15   Ibid.
16   *Margaret Fuller, Critic: Writings from the New-York Tribune, 1844-1846* by Judith Mattson Bean and Joel Myerson (Columbia University Press, 2000).
17   Ibid.
18   Ibid.
19   Ibid.
20   Capper, *The Public Years.*
21   Von Mehren.
22   Ibid.
23   Ibid.
24   Fuller, *Memoirs.*
25   Capper, *The Private Years.*
26   Ibid.

(This essay was excerpted from a display
I created for Margaret Fuller's Bicentennial.)


"If I could talk to her, I would just say 'thank you' and let her know that every African American artist knows her name."

*—Denise Ward Brown, sculptor, on Edmonia Lewis*

# Edmonia Lewis

**(1845–1907)**

---

## Her Achievements

- First African American to earn an international reputation as a sculptor
- First Native American and first African American female sculptor
- Used her art to influence the public's attitudes toward slavery and the plight of Native Americans
- Owned successful studios in Boston and Rome in spite of nineteenth century racism and sexism
- Did her own carving to avoid being accused of fraud
- 2002: She is listed in *100 Greatest African Americans: A Biographical Encyclopedia*

---

**Her Story**

As one biographer writes about Edmonia, "She boldly breached barriers of race, ethnicity, gender, religion, and class around the time of the Civil War and Reconstruction, an era when prejudices against these minorities were particularly virulent ... Her success spurred generations of artists and expanded the horizons of black feminists as a pioneer of racial identity." That's pretty impressive! So, who was this groundbreaking artist?[1]

Mary Edmonia Lewis was born about 1845, presumably in upstate New York (her birth records have never been found). Her father was Haitian; her mother, who was of Ojibwe (or Chippewa) and African American descent, was known as an artist of traditional crafts. According to Edmonia, in an interview she gave to Lydia Maria Child for the abolitionist newspaper the *Liberator*, her Native American name was "Wild Fire."[2]

Sadly, both of Edmonia's parents died when she was about nine, and she and her older brother, Samuel, went to live with their mother's sisters selling baskets and other Native American crafts to tourists.

As a teenager, Edmonia began studying art at Oberlin College in Ohio, which was one of the first colleges in the United States to admit women and people of different ethnicities. As she once said about choosing to become an artist, "Well, it was a strange selection for a poor girl to make, wasn't it? I suppose it was in me ... I became almost crazy to make something like the things which fascinated me."[3]

Edmonia was studying at Oberlin when the Civil War broke out. At school, a racist and violent incident took place when she was accused of poisoning two white female students who had become severely ill during an outing. Edmonia was severely beaten, accused of the crime, and made to stand trial. Luckily, she was found innocent thanks, in part, to the efforts of John Mercer Langston, the only practicing African American lawyer at Oberlin.

## Art

With her brother's financial help, Edmonia moved to Boston in 1863 to study with the great sculptor Edward August Brackett. She carried with her letters of introduction to some of the leading abolitionists of the day, black and white, including William Lloyd Garrison. According to the historian and Edmonia Lewis scholar Marilyn Richardson, "She was soon advertising portrait busts and terra-cotta medallions of champions of the antislavery cause, including Senator Charles Sumner, Maria Weston Chapman, the martyred John Brown, and the black Sergeant William H. Carney, a hero of the 54th Massachusetts Regiment in the 1863 Civil War battle at Fort Wagner." Bostonians wanted to collect these beautifully executed abolitionist works carved by an African American woman.[4]

Edmonia's financial success from her depictions of Robert Gould Shaw, the white commanding officer of the 54th Regiment (the country's first regiment of African American men), helped fund her first trip to Italy—at age twenty-one—where she settled in 1866. From now on, Edmonia would be a true international artist, traveling regularly between Rome, Boston, and other American cities where she exhibited her work.

In Rome, where Edmonia had more freedom as a woman and as an African American artist, she was surrounded by other Boston expatriate artists including Charlotte Cushman, Louisa Lander, Anne Whitney, Harriet Hosmer, Hiram Power, and William Wetmore Story. As Edmonia herself explained: "I was practically driven to Rome, in order to obtain the opportunities for art culture, and to find a social atmosphere where I was not constantly reminded of my color. The land of liberty had no room for a colored sculptor."[5]

In Italy Edmonia found a "real republic," where people "left their race prejudices at home." She stayed there for the rest of her life," writes Dr. Pat McNamara of American Catholic University. In Rome, Edmonia practiced Catholicism, and was possibly raised in that church, setting her apart from her fellow Protestant expatriates. Although most of her religious art does not survive, during Edmonia's time she brought "a uniquely African perspective to her religious work," writes McNamara, explaining, "One critic, for example, observed that in her sculpture of the Magi, the preeminent figure was the African king, rather than the Caucasian or the Asiatic." Edmonia herself once stated, "I have a strong sympathy for all women who have struggled and suffered. For this reason the Virgin Mary is very dear to me."[6]

Edmonia did well in Rome. As Marilyn Richardson writes, "Lewis's work was much in demand. Her studio, listed in the best guidebooks, was a fashionable stop for travelers on the mid-nineteenth-century version of the Grand Tour.

Some visitors commissioned portrait busts of themselves or family members. Others ordered her biblical, literary, historical, or idealized classical figures to adorn their mantels and front parlors." Richardson also points out that as an African American woman whose talent could be questioned if she hired assistants, she did all of her own carving.[7]

## Politics

Edmonia's depictions of Native Americans "were an immediate success," Richardson writes, due to the international popularity of Henry Wadsworth Longfellow's poem "The Song of Hiawatha." Richardson points out that collectors were eager to have a copy of Edmonia's figures that were inspired by his poems because they had been carved by someone of Ojibway descent. The Smithsonian Institution wrote about her sculpture, "Her works were infused with both personal relevance and timely human rights issues ... Her sculptures were displayed from Boston to Chicago to San Francisco as well as in her studio in Rome."[8]

In 1868, Edmonia completed "Forever Free" and sent it to abolitionists in Boston. The same year, she sculpted "Hagar in the Wilderness," using a Biblical story to raise the issue of freedom. At the time, because she did not have a buyer for the piece, she rented an exhibition room in Chicago and advertised special viewing times for twenty-five cents. She eventually sold her work for $6,000. After, Dr. Harriot Kezia Hunt commissioned a life-size statue of Hygieia for her future gravesite at Mount Auburn Cemetery in Cambridge, Massachusetts. Edmonia created an altar piece for St. Francis Xavier Church in Baltimore.[9]

During the next several years, Edmonia completed commissions, especially busts and medallion portraits, and won praise and awards including a gold medal for "Lincoln, Asleep" at the Academy of Arts and Sciences in Naples. In 1873, according to a biographer, "Edmonia was the first internationally renowned woman sculptor to exhibit in San Francisco and San Jose, where she won significant praise. She showed "Lincoln, Asleep and Awake," "Cupid Caught," and "The Marriage of Hiawatha," and sold most of the pieces. The Friends of San Jose Library purchased the Lincoln bust, where it remains to this day. She also exhibited works in St. Paul, Minnesota, the following year. Upon returning to Rome, she found her artist friends diligently working on pieces for the Philadelphia Centennial Exposition. Edmonia spent the next year working, too, on what would become her greatest triumph."[10]

Edmonia's triumph, shown in 1876, was "The Death of Cleopatra" for the Centennial Exposition in Philadelphia, which portrayed a strong, courageous queen in the moments before her death. The American statesman J.S. Ingraham described the two-ton marble statue as "the most remarkable piece of sculpture in the American section" of the Exposition." It caused a sensation. The following year, President Ulysses S. Grant asked her to sculpt his portrait, which she did. She created "The Veiled Bride of Spring" for exhibitions in New York and Cincinnati, busts of leading Catholic men and the African American poet Phillis Wheatley, a statue of the Holy Virgin, and an altar piece for a church in Baltimore. When Frederick Douglass visited Edmonia in Rome in 1887, he found her "cheerful and happy and successful."[11]

Edmonia exhibited "Hiawatha" and "Phillis Wheatley" at the World's Columbian Exposition in Chicago in 1893, and her bust of the abolitionist Charles Sumner at the Atlanta World's Fair in 1895. Unfortunately, though, just at this time, public taste in art was shifting to Paris and Lewis's neoclassic style declined in popularity.[12]

What happened to Edmonia next is unclear. The last years of her life remain shrouded in mystery. It was thought that she died in Rome, or in California. Instead, in 2010, Marilyn Richardson was able to document Edmonia's death in the Hammersmith area of London in 1907.[13]

Edmonia's last residence was located ten minutes from the Catholic church she attended. The church stood in the midst of a "colony of Catholics" that included a convent of teaching sisters, schools, an almshouse, and St. Mary's Orphanage. According to a biographer, "Her will specified a Catholic funeral and burial at Kensal Green, London. It named a Catholic priest as her executor and main beneficiary. At the time of Edmonia's death, her estate was worth about sixty thousand of today's dollars."[14]

After her death, the poet Vivian Shipley wrote:

"If her grave were found and marked today
the tombstone would have no hyphen, one title:
SCULPTOR."

The sculptor Denise Ward Brown wrote:

"If I could talk to her, I would just say 'thank you'
and let her know that every African American
artist knows her name."

She did not live, she did not work in vain."[15]

Today, Edmonia Lewis's works are owned by the Smithsonian American Art Museum, Harvard University, Howard University, Oberlin College, San José Library, and several other American museums, libraries, and private collections. She continues to inspire female, African American, and Native American artists alike with her courage, dedication, and artistic excellence.

Edmonia Lewis's most famous political sculptures include:

- "Forever Free"
- "The Freed Woman and Her Child"
- "Colonel Robert Gould Shaw"
- "Henry Wadsworth Longfellow"
- "John Brown"
- "Charles Sumner"
- "Lincoln, Asleep and Awake"
- "Phillis Wheatley"
- "Marriage of Hiawatha"
- "Hiawatha"
- "Minnehaha"
- "The Old Arrowmaker and His Daughter"
- "The Death of Cleopatra"

## Her Faith in Action

What's fascinating about Edmonia Lewis is her cultural background as part Native American combined with the fact that she appears to have been raised Catholic. For years, historians have argued about when she embraced Catholicism, but current thinking has her Catholic early on and not a convert later in life as was previously thought.

Edmonia's own statements add to the confusion about what was true—on purpose! She was a master at manipulating the media and presenting an intriguing, mysterious image of herself.

Mid-career, she wrote, "How strange the Great Spirit has led me on without father or mother," acknowledging her Native American roots. She felt a deep tie to Nature, once writing, "There is nothing so beautiful as the free forest. To catch a fish when you are hungry, cut the boughs of a tree, make fire to roast it, and eat it in the open air, is the greatest of all luxuries. I would not stay a week pent up in cities, if it were not for my passion for Art." Recalling her childhood, she wrote, "I was ... declared to be wild—they could do nothing with me. Often they said to me, 'Here is your book, the book of Nature; come and study it' ... I thought of returning to wild life again; but my love of sculpture forbade it."[16]

Later in life, as a Catholic, she made statements like, "I have a strong sympathy for all women who have struggled and suffered. For this reason the Virgin Mary is very dear to me."

Edmonia Lewis clearly had a very strong sense of herself as a trail blazer and role model for African American women, for Native American women, and for women sculptors. I think it's safe to assume that her faith in her God-given talents, and her ability to push through barriers, gave her the strength to keep at it. She knew she was here for a reason. In a humorous moment, she wrote: "I kept up my pluck with a bible and brandy bottle beside my bed, so that if one gave out she might take to the other."

About living and working in Italy, she wrote:

"It would have done your heart good to see what a friendly welcome I received ... How much I have thought about that encouraging reception. It is a great example for the US Government to follow in her treatment of a poor people struggling to rise out of degradation."

"I was practically driven to Rome In order to obtain the opportunities for art culture, and to find a social atmosphere where I was not constantly reminded of my color. The land of liberty had not room for a colored sculptor."

"My first thought was for my poor father's people, how I could do them good in a very small way ... I am going back to Italy to do something for the race—something that will excite the admiration of the other races of the earth."

"I shall never live in America."

Primarily, Edmonia Lewis's works of art divide into two categories: political and religious. Among her religious works of art were altar pieces, statues of the Virgin Mary, and images from Biblical stories. At the end of her life, Edmonia chose to live near a Catholic community in London. Her will specified a Catholic funeral and burial at Kensal Green, London. It named a Catholic priest as her executor and main beneficiary. Clearly, her artistic work, her personal life, and her chosen religion were intertwined.

## Sites to Visit in Massachusetts

Studio of Edmonia Lewis (site of)
Corner of Bromfield and Tremont Streets
Boston, MA 02108
*Edmonia studied sculpture here starting in 1863,
and opened her own studio.*

## Resources

"Hiawatha in Rome: Edmonia Lewis and Figures from
Longfellow" by Marilyn Richardson for *Antiques and Fine
Art* magazine, 2012.

Websites:
*Search for Edmonia Lewis at:*
Boston Women's Heritage Trail
Edmonialewis.com
Patheos.com
Womeninhistory.com

## Notes to the Biographical Sketch

1    Edmonialewis.com
2    Womeninhistory.com
3    Edmonialewis.com
4    "Hiawatha in Rome: Edmonia Lewis and Figures
     from Longfellow" by Marilyn Richardson for *Antiques
     and Fine Art* magazine, 2012.
5    Edmonialewis.com
6    patheos.com, and edmonialewis.com
7    Richardson.
8    Ibid.
9    Womeninhistory.com
10   Womeninhistory.com
11   Womeninhistory.com
12   Womeninhistory.com, and Richardson.
13   Edmonialewis.com
14   Ibid.

15 Ibid.
16 Ibid., and for the rest of the Faith section.

"The idea of the incapability of women is ... totally inadmissible ... To argue against facts, is indeed contending with both wind and tide; and, borne down by accumulating examples, conviction of the utility of the present plans will pervade the public mind, and not a dissenting voice will be heard.

Yes, in this younger world, "the Rights of Women" begin to be understood ... we are ready to contend for the quantity, as well as the quality, of mind ... I may be accused of enthusiasm; but such is my confidence in THE SEX, that I expect to see our young women forming a new era in female history."

—*Judith Sargent Murray*

# Judith Sargent Murray

## (1751–1820)

---

### Her Achievements

- First to claim female equality in the public prints
- First woman in America to self-publish a book
- First American to have a play produced in Boston
- Most important female essayist of the New American Republic
- Declared "Ablest poet" by *Massachusetts Magazine*
- Earliest known American Universalist author
- Co-founder of a female academy
- The only eighteenth century woman known to have kept letter books in a consistent manner

---

**Her Story**
(This essay is reprinted, with modifications, from my book *Mingling Souls Upon Paper: An Eighteenth-Century Love Story.*)

The Gloucester, Massachusetts, of Judith Sargent Murray's childhood was a thriving colonial seaport in "His Britannik Majesty's" empire populated by hardy, independent-minded, townspeople. Many families, like the Sargents and Saunderses, had immigrated from England in the seventeenth century to pursue economic opportunities. By 1751, the year Judith was born, they had achieved considerable wealth from exporting fish, lumber, and other commodities to England and the West Indies and importing valuable goods. They were distinguished, engaged citizens whose trade activities exposed them to people and ideas from other parts of the world. Judith Sargent was born on May 5 into these two families, the oldest child of Winthrop Sargent and Judith Saunders Sargent, only four of whose children survived to adulthood.[1]

Judith's parents provided a typical education for a merchant-class daughter—reading, writing, and training in the domestic skills of sewing and household management. At the same time, though, the Sargents had hired a tutor for their son Winthrop to prepare him for Harvard College. Judith was keenly aware of the differences between their educations. She wanted to learn more, and under her own initiative read books of history, geography, literature, philosophy, and theology found in the Sargent family library. Judith became an avid reader and a "scribbler" from an early age, writing poetry, historical essays, and letters to family members and close friends.[2]

Like most children in Gloucester, Judith was raised in
First Parish Church whose Congregational ministers ruled
religious and civic life. She was taught to be virtuous,
benevolent, and well-behaved to avoid God's anger.
Judith learned that only a few people were predestined for
heaven, while most would spend eternity in hell. It was not
a particularly optimistic outlook, but Judith's religious life
was balanced by her family's self-confident business and
political pursuits.

Judith fulfilled the one role expected of her when she
married John Stevens at the age of eighteen. She had
chosen well and appropriately, selecting the son of a
prominent Gloucester family. The young couple resided
with John's parents until they could build a house of their
own, allowing Judith to live within a short distance of the
Sargent and Saunders homes. Their new home would be
built in the adjacent lot.[3]

At about the same time, Judith's father read James
Relly's book on universal salvation, *Union, or, A Treatise
of the Consanguinity and Affinity between Christ and
His Church*. Winthrop Sargent was intrigued with the
scriptural interpretation Relly articulated, and he began to
host gatherings in his home to discuss the new theology.
It was a radical departure from traditional doctrine, and
Judith was among those who embraced Relly's hopeful,
egalitarian view of the worlds here and beyond.
In 1774, when Winthrop Sargent learned that the English
Universalist preacher John Murray was lecturing in
Boston, he invited him to visit Gloucester. On November
3, John Murray presented himself at the Sargent family
home where Judith met him for the first time. Judith asked

John if he would agree to engage in a correspondence (specifically, to "mingle souls upon paper"), and he accepted. While John moved to Gloucester shortly thereafter, he traveled frequently to other parts of New England and depended on Judith's accounts of life in his adopted town while he was away.[4]

At first, Judith's letters were filled with theological inquiry, but soon she was reporting fearful goings-on in Gloucester such as when British warships appeared off the coast in 1775 and Judith and her family retreated for their safety to Chebacco Parish, Ipswich, that winter. Her Loyalist uncle, Epes Sargent, later one of John Murray's most influential supporters, was forced by angry separatists to leave town for Boston.

These were tense times in Gloucester, and not simply because of the war. John Murray's Universalist supporters, including Judith, faced a different kind of battle in 1775 when they were threatened with expulsion from First Parish Church for not attending. John Murray was accused of being a British spy, and he quickly accepted a post as Army chaplain to prove his loyalty to the American cause. During his absence, Judith kept him apprised of Gloucester's desperate poverty while the port was closed. When John returned in 1776, he successfully raised funds to alleviate Gloucester's distress.

By 1778, war activities had moved south, and now the leadership of First Parish took action against the Universalists of Gloucester by suspending Judith Sargent Stevens, Winthrop Sargent, Epes Sargent (who had returned to Gloucester), and others from the church.

Instead of backing down, the Universalists, including Judith, signed Articles of Association the following year to create a new religious society: the Independent Church of Christ. Soon after, the Gloucester Universalists built their own meeting house and dedicated the building on Christmas Day 1780, calling John Murray as their pastor. Even though Judith was in Boston at the time nursing her father through smallpox, she delighted in the Universalists' significant achievement.

Judith quickly found herself in the role of religious educator for Gloucester's growing number of Universalist children. She had recently adopted two of her husband's orphaned nieces, Anna and Mary Plummer, and temporarily took in a third little cousin, Polly Odell, as well. Before long, Universalist parents urged Judith to write down the lessons she was teaching. She complied, and in 1782 Judith published a Universalist catechism that is today considered the earliest writing by an American Universalist woman. The pamphlet included Judith's first public assertion of male and female equality, a hallmark of Universalism.

In the same year, the Universalists' defiance of First Parish led the ruling ministers to seize valuable goods from Winthrop Sargent, Epes Sargent, and others to sell at public auction. Even though the Universalists had formed their own organization, they were still expected to support the established church—which they refused to do. The Universalists persuaded John Murray, as their leader, to bring their case before the Massachusetts Supreme Judicial Court and argue for the right to separate from First Parish and support their own church. Eventually, in 1785 and 1786, the court ruled in favor of the Universalists and freedom of religion.

## Change

Judith's life took a dramatic turn in 1786 when John
Stevens revealed just how much his debts had
accumulated since wartime trade embargoes and a
series of storms had destroyed his cargo and ships. He
was embroiled in discussions with his creditors to obtain
leniency and avoid debtor's prison. Even John Murray
stepped in to negotiate on his behalf. Judith, her husband,
and Anna Plummer spent the winter of 1785–6 literally
locked inside their home to keep John Stevens safe
from the sheriff. That spring, as a desperate last resort,
John Stevens secretly left Gloucester for St. Eustacius in
the West Indies where he hoped to restore his financial
standing by participating in international trade.

Her husband's departure left Judith ill and depressed.
Following her physicians' advice, she agreed to a journey
in the countryside with Anna Plummer, escorted by John
Murray. For the first time, Judith saw John preach to
crowds of hundreds of people at a time. Until then, she
had not fully appreciated his stature and the effect he
could have on so many "hearers" from all walks of life.

Judith learned of her husband's death the following
year and resigned herself to life as a widow. But John
Murray had other ideas: at the close of 1787 he asked
Judith to marry him. At the time, John had made plans
to sail for England in January on the advice of his
Universalist supporters. His ministry had been challenged
again by First Parish, he had even been threatened,
and Winthrop Sargent suggested he leave Gloucester

while the Universalists secured a legal ruling from the Massachusetts legislature.

Judith waited many long and apprehensive weeks for a positive decision from the legislature and for her future husband's safe return. When the Universalists received word in their favor upholding the legality of John's ministry a few months later, Judith immediately wrote to John with the good news and he sailed for Gloucester that fall. They married in Salem, Massachusetts, on October 6, 1788. Despite her brother Winthrop's inexplicable disapproval of her marriage, Judith explained to an aunt that John Murray was the "election of [her] heart."[5]

Before long, Judith was pregnant with their first baby. After a childless marriage with John Stevens, she was elated. She was thirty-nine years old and had just about given up hope. But in August 1789, the little boy they had planned to name Fitz Winthrop was stillborn. Judith nearly died as well, and faced a lengthy, painful recovery.

## Career

While she was bedridden, Judith wrote poetry to submit to the *Massachusetts Magazine* using the pen name "Constantia." Her 1784 essay, "Desultory Thoughts upon the Utility of Encouraging a Degree of Self-Complacency, Especially in Female Bosoms," had been well received in the *Gentleman and Lady's Town and Country Magazine*, and she hoped to develop an even wider audience for her political and creative ideas. Along with poetry, the following year, 1790, she submitted what would become her landmark essay. "On the Equality of the Sexes," appeared in the March and April issues of the

*Massachusetts Magazine*, closely followed by "On the Domestic Education of Children" in May.

Later that year, when Judith embarked on a six-month journey to Philadelphia with John, she experienced a dizzying array of people, places, events, and ideas through the eyes of an acclaimed essayist. Her meetings with President George Washington, Martha Washington, Vice President John Adams, Abigail Adams, and other dignitaries must have heightened her desire to participate in national conversations about citizenship, virtue, philanthropy, female education, and the role of women in the New Republic. Judith knew that as a woman, writing was the only way to have a voice.

When Judith returned home, she was pregnant again at the age of forty-one. This time, though, her maternal hopes were realized when she gave birth on August 22, 1791, to a healthy baby girl they named Julia Maria. Judith's contentment overflowed that year when the *Massachusetts Magazine* declared "Constantia" one of its ablest poets. Despite John's many absences when he was invited to preach outside of Gloucester, Judith now enjoyed a happy family life and a promising literary career, which she was about to advance significantly.

Her decision to create a new column in 1792 for the *Massachusetts Magazine* stemmed from the knowledge that her friends and family knew "Constantia's" real identity. This time, in choosing a pen name, she settled on a masculine identity as "Mr. Gleaner" to engage more male readers in her ideas and avoid being dismissed as a female writer. "The Gleaner" addressed many of the political and social issues that were close to Judith's heart, and "he" developed quite a following. A few months later, as "Constantia," Judith created a second column for the *Massachusetts Magazine* called "The Repository," which included shorter, more reflective, and even Universalist pieces.

## Boston

In 1794, after John had been ordained as the minister of Boston's Universalist congregation, the family moved to Franklin Place, Boston, where Judith would be in the center of New England cultural and political activity. News of Judith's arrival prompted Thomas Paine, the editor of one of Boston's newspapers, the *Federal Orrery*, to prevail upon her to create a new column. Judith agreed, and submitted five installments of "The Reaper." In this series, Judith investigated lessons regarding character and virtue that she had "reaped" from real life. To her dismay, Paine not only edited her work but changed words and sentences altogether. Judith refused to submit more columns, not knowing that Thomas Paine would later cause trouble for the Murrays.

Thomas Paine's mean-spiritedness surfaced in 1795 and 1796, when Judith's plays were performed at the Boston Theatre on Federal Street making her the first American—male or female—to be so honored. *The Medium, or Happy Tea-Party* (1795) and *The Traveller Returned* (1796) were comedies about class structure, patriotism, and virtue, and they featured strong female characters. Thomas Paine, himself a hopeful playwright, perhaps resented Judith's success. He not only denounced *Traveller*, he accused John Murray of writing it and serving as the male pen behind Judith's literary efforts. The public spectacle dismayed John's conservative congregation, but John defended his wife's abilities by publishing letters in Boston's weekly newspapers.

## Gleaner

In 1796, Julia Maria was a talkative, precocious five-year-old whose early education Judith oversaw herself. Julia Maria used to scold her mother for not providing a brother or sister. Suddenly, out of the blue, Judith's brother Winthrop wrote to her from the Ohio Territory where he held a high-ranking government position. He told Judith about his infant illegitimate daughter, Caroline Augusta, whom he wanted Judith to raise in Boston. Judith agreed unhesitatingly, pleased with the chance to provide a sister for Julia Maria, but Winthrop was never able to persuade Caroline Augusta's mother to relinquish her daughter.

Along with her role as a mother, Judith's domestic duties included managing the family finances. She often had to plead with the Boston Universalist congregation for John's salary. Her decision in 1796 to produce a book was as much to generate income as it was to achieve real literary fame. A shrewd businesswoman, she secured early support from President George Washington and Vice President John Adams (she also dedicated the book to Adams) for her "indigenous," meaning, American, production. When the two men agreed to her request, she used their names to attract subscribers from the highest ranks of civic, military, business, and academic circles. When *The Gleaner* appeared in 1798, Judith became the first woman in America to self-publish a book. Two years later, American novelists Henry Sherburne and Sally Wood, among others, praised Judith for *The Gleaner's*

timeless importance to social and political thought,
and they thanked her for the doors she had opened for
emerging American writers.

Young people were very much Judith's focus at home
along with those she hoped would read *The Gleaner*.
In the early 1800s, her brother Winthrop sent his
stepdaughter, Anna Williams, to live at Franklin Place.
He sent his sons and stepsons to academies in Billerica,
Massachusetts, and Exeter, New Hampshire, as well.
Later, "the boys" attended Harvard. Throughout her
nephews' years away from home, Judith visited and
wrote to them, and hosted them during school vacations.
Judith's reputation as an educator expanded still further
in 1802, when Judith Saunders, a cousin, and Clementine
Beach asked Judith to support their new female academy
in Dorchester, Massachusetts, where they hoped
to provide the kind of education Judith had always
championed for girls.

During these years, Judith published poetry in the *Boston
Weekly Magazine* under a new pen name, "Honora
Martesia." In 1805 she wrote a third play, *The African*,
which was inexplicably rejected by a critic during rehearsal
and whose manuscript has never been found.

## Stroke

Judith's life changed abruptly in 1809 when John Murray's
tireless traveling and recurring illnesses caught up with
him. A massive stroke left the right side of his body numb,
incapacitating John for the rest of his life. Although his
mind was alert and he could still speak, he could no longer
travel, preach, or take care of his family. The Murrays

were already struggling to make ends meet; Judith was shaken. The Universalist congregation hired a private nurse and sent male members of the congregation each day to move John within his apartment or out to a waiting carriage. Even so, Judith was John's constant bedside companion and she marveled at his patience and good nature.

Having lost the services of their pastor, the Boston Universalists installed the Reverend Edward Mitchell in John's place, much to Judith's delight. He was a Rellyan Universalist from New York who could, hopefully, return the church to more traditional Universalist theology. Ten years earlier, John had inadvertently allowed the Reverend Hosea Ballou to preach in his pulpit. The Unitarian views Ballou espoused at that time were not at all in keeping with the teachings of James Relly, and the Boston congregation had been in theological disarray ever since. Now, perhaps, Edward Mitchell could help. Unfortunately, though, he left after only a short time and Judith found herself refusing to attend church and "sanction by her presence" the Universalists' theological shift.

The same year of Edward Mitchell's departure, 1812, Judith helped John edit and publish a collection of his writings titled *Letters and Sketches of Sermons*. They hoped the book would solidify John's historic role in Universalism and bring them income. While the work was in process, Julia Maria married Adam Lewis Bingaman, a Harvard graduate from Natchez, Mississippi, who had boarded with the Murrays for a short time. In 1813, Julia Maria gave birth to her parents' first grandchild, Charlotte, and both Judith and John were enchanted by the baby's playful presence.

But war with Great Britain disrupted the Murrays' family life as investments failed and American troops arrived in Boston to protect the port. Judith and John feared for their safety, frustrated by the difficulty with physically removing John from Boston if the British set fire to their city as they had done to Washington. Although they survived the hostilities and looked forward to resuming a peaceful life together, John Murray died in 1815 after almost six years of painful confinement. Judith was bereft, having spent forty-one years as his devoted friend and wife. But John had longed to escape the "prison" of his incapacitated body, and she knew they would see each other again in the next world. She was probably relieved on his behalf.

The Universalists held two services for John, one in Gloucester and the other in Boston, where a long procession through the city ended with John's interment in the Sargent family tomb at Granary Burying Ground. Within a month, Universalist friends approached Judith to complete the autobiography John had abandoned in 1774, and she turned to Edward Mitchell for assistance. Judith published *Records of the Life of the Rev. John Murray* in 1816, hoping again to preserve her husband's legacy.

Judith would have preferred to end her days at Franklin Place in the same bed she had shared with her husband. But Adam Lewis Bingaman, who had long since returned to Natchez, had legal control over his wife and daughter and Judith could not bear a separation from her offspring. In 1818, Adam sent word to Boston that he was on his way to escort his family to Natchez. Among the items Judith packed were some of John's papers and the twenty volumes of letter books she had produced throughout her adult life—blank volumes into which she had deliberately copied her correspondence to family members, friends, and business acquaintances.

Very little is known about Judith's time in Natchez, where she lived for the last years of her life in the Bingaman family mansion, Oak Point. By then, her eyesight had deteriorated and it is possible she stopped writing letters because none have been found and her letter books end with a letter penned from Boston. In Natchez, Judith was reunited with her beloved brother Winthrop, his children, and stepchildren who no doubt enjoyed spending time with the same "Aunt Murray" who had so lovingly guided them through their education. Judith Sargent Murray died on June 9, 1820, at the age of sixty-nine, and lies buried in the Bingaman family cemetery at Fatherland Plantation. On her mother's gravestone, Julia Maria inscribed, "Dear Spirit, the monumental stone can never speak thy worth."[6]

## Her Faith in Action

Judith's leadership role in the early days of Universalism have many of today's Unitarian Universalist historians and ministers convinced that she was at least partly responsible for women being allowed into the Universalist ministry so early on. It's hard to disagree. She really went out on a limb to follow her chosen faith, and took risks. It was the same courage she displayed in her writing —courage born out of faith.

When Judith was growing up in Gloucester, there was one church and everyone was expected to attend. The Congregational/Calvinist theology she learned was not quite as dismal as what Anne Bradstreet heard in the previous century, but the Gloucester ministers certainly preached about God's anger, predestination for a chosen few, hell for everyone else, and the necessity of behaving well just in case. Judith's father, Winthrop Sargent, rejected this dark interpretation of the Bible and so did Judith. While people elsewhere in the colonies were also reading James Relly's book on Universalist theology, it was the Gloucester Universalists who institutionalized Universalism.

Judith embraced Universalism to her core. Everything she wrote and did is tied to the ideas of equality, the interconnectedness of the Universal "family of man" and Nature, and to a loving God who promised salvation for the faithful. Adding her signature to the Universalists' 1779 Articles of Faith, resulting in suspension from First Church, was gutsy. She was in the company of family members, but it was a courageous act nonetheless.

Judith's 1782 published catechism for children opens with a statement about male and female equality in the eyes of God. This work, thought to be the earliest by an American Universalist woman, established Judith as a leader and teacher. It was published in New Hampshire and Connecticut, and while there is no way of knowing how many copies were distributed it no doubt "got around."

Judith's unwavering belief in Universalist principles extended to John Murray, and she was his faithful supporter, promoter, and some time secretary, long before they were married. When she began to write for publication in 1784, initiating a hugely successful literary career, her writing was filled with the Universalist themes of equality, virtue, philanthropy, Nature, and interconnectedness. Did she help John Murray write his sermons? We don't know the answer, but he certainly respected her and they must have exchanged ideas.

From Judith's letters we know that she and John engaged in lengthy theological discussions on paper. Her intellectual and spiritual inquisitiveness are clear. In him, she had found a mentor and pastor. From her letters, we also know that she counseled people who were dying, who had lost a loved one, or who faced some kind of diversity. She reached out to young people, and advised them on their "career of life," as she called it, or an impending marriage. In writing, and in person, she truly put her faith into action.

## Sites to Visit in Massachusetts

Home of Judith Sargent Murray
Sargent House Museum
42 Middle Street
Gloucester, MA 01930
*Judith lived here from 1782 to 1794, with her first husband, John Stevens, and her second husband, John Murray. The house is open for guided tours.*

Home of Judith Sargent Murray (site of)
Franklin Place/The Tontine Crescent
Franklin and Arch Streets
Boston, MA 02108
*Judith lived here from 1794 to 1818. There is a historic marker on the opposite side of Franklin Street.*

Independent Christian Church (Unitarian Universalist)
10 Church Street
Gloucester, MA 01930
*This was the second church built by the Gloucester Universalists. Built in 1809, it's a big step up from the first, very modest meeting house from 1780!*

## Resources

*Judith Sargent Murray Papers*, available on microfilm from the Mississippi Department of Archives and History, Jackson, MS. Also check your local library.

*"I Am Jealous for the Honor of Our Sex:" A Brief Biography of Judith Sargent Murray* by Bonnie Hurd Smith (Hurd Smith Communications, 2011).

*Letters of Loss & Love: Judith Sargent Murray Papers, Letter Book 3* by Bonnie Hurd Smith (Hurd Smith Communications, 2009).

*Mingling Souls Upon Paper: An Eighteenth-Century Love Story* by Bonnie Hurd Smith (Hurd Smith Communications, 2007).

*The Letters I Left Behind: Judith Sargent Murray Papers, Letter Book 10* by Bonnie Hurd Smith (Hurd Smith Communications, 2005).

*From Gloucester to Philadelphia in 1790: Observations, Thoughts, and Anecdotes from the Letters of Judith Sargent Murray* by Bonnie Hurd Smith (Curious Traveller Press, 1996).

Websites:

*Search for Judith Sargent Murray at:*
Boston Women's Heritage Trail
Dictionary of Unitarian Universalist Biography
Harvard Square Library
Judith Sargent Murray Society
Oxford University's Anthology of American Literature

## Notes to the Biographical Sketch

1   Judith frequently referred to King George in this way.
2   Judith Sargent Murray to Rev. William Emerson,
    21 November 1805.
3   Today, this house is the Sargent House Museum.
4   Judith Sargent Stevens to John Murray,
    14 November 1774.
5   Judith Sargent Murray to Mary Turner Sargent,
    13 October 1788.
6   Judith's numerous nieces and nephews wrote letters
    to her in which they addressed her as "Aunt Murray";
    Julia Maria Murray's inscription on her mother's grave
    stone has been transcribed by several visitors to the
    grave site including Rev. Gordon Gibson, who found
    Judith's letter books.

"To contemplate the Spirit in ourselves, and in
our fellow man, is obviously the only means of
understanding social duty, and quickening within
ourselves a wise Humanity—In general terms,—
Contemplation of Spirit is the first principle of
Human Culture; the foundation
of Self-education."

*—Elizabeth Peabody*

# Elizabeth Palmer Peabody

## (1804–1894)

## Her Achievements

- Founder of kindergartens in America
- First woman publisher in Boston
- Owner of successful book store and lending library in Boston, where Margaret Fuller's "Conversations" for women took place
- Leading Transcendentalist and Unitarian; editor and publisher of the *Dial*, the Transcendentalist newspaper
- Author
- Teacher, including at Bronson Alcott's Temple School
- Along with her sisters, Mary Peabody Mann and Sophia Peabody Hawthorne, considered a leading figure in nineteenth century American Romanticism

## Her Story

(This essay is excerpted from a Unitarian sermon I delivered at the First Church in Salem, Unitarian, in Salem, Massachusetts, for Elizabeth's bicentennial.)

A few years ago, I was asked to deliver a sermon at my local Unitarian church for Elizabeth Peabody's 200th birthday. I titled it, "I Must Be Myself and Act" because those words, famously written by her all those years ago, still ring true—and it's what Elizabeth Peabody did throughout her long and productive life.

Neither one is easy—being yourself, and acting. To be yourself involves figuring out what YOU believe, and not what others have told you to believe, and then to act on it. In Elizabeth Peabody's time, as in ours, acting on one's convictions, acting on who we are, can have consequences. It can mean risking a great deal.

On top of all of this, especially if you were born two hundred years ago, you ran the risk of being defined by others, and you really had no control over it. Stories about Elizabeth being overweight, not always neat in appearance, and sometimes absent-minded have been perpetuated and embellished, leading even to Henry James's fictional character of Miss Birdseye in his book *The Bostonians*.

But in her bicentennial year, we reclaimed Elizabeth because she was, in fact, a woman of extraordinary achievements: she was a teacher, editor, publisher, translator, historian, bookseller, correspondent, and essayist. She was gifted in linguistics, literature, history, theology, philosophy, and geography, and every single one of us living in the United States is a beneficiary of her work in early childhood education.[1]

## Foundations

Elizabeth Palmer Peabody was born two hundred years ago in Billerica, Massachusetts. On both the Palmer and Peabody sides of her family, as my grandmother would say, she was descended from good New England stock— not wealthy, but well educated and respectable.

Both of her parents were tutors, and had worked together at the Franklin Academy in North Andover. Her mother ran a school from the family home, while she encouraged her husband to study medicine and earn more than a school teacher's salary, which he was doing by 1808 when the family moved to a rented house in Salem, Massachusetts. Elizabeth's mother's school was rigorous and progressive, and she did not differentiate between what the boys and girls were reading. Her example of how she treated children would serve Elizabeth well. As she wrote many years later, she was "pre-natally educated for the profession which has been the passionate pursuit of my life."[2]

Elizabeth's determination to "be herself" started early. She has been described as a precocious girl, which always amuses me because it means she wasn't thinking or doing what she was told. As her biographer, Bruce Ronda, explains, she grew up in a family "where women, not men, were the dominant intellectual and emotional forces" and where her parenting responsibilities, as the oldest child, started early.[3]

From a very early age, she was determined to have a "life of the mind." She was self-reflective, and would always be engaged in an endless quest "to take the measure of her interior life," as her most recent biographer, Megan Marshall, explains.

This "precocious girl" was spiritually hungry, having been born at a time when Calvinist orthodoxy and more progressive theology were strongly at odds with each other. When her mother took her to hear the Unitarian Reverend William Ellery Channing preach at Salem's North Church when she was just seven years old, it changed her life forever. Channing was filling Thomas Barnard's pulpit for the day, and he had a profound effect on young Elizabeth who was already trying to determine her own theology. During this time she also heard her parents heatedly discussing Noah Worcester's anti-Trinitarian book, *Bible News*, and she realized that religion was "a subject of enquiry and dispute ... not quite a settled thing that we must believe the popular system of theology."[4]

## Religious Inquiry

Along with early ideas of Unitarianism that had come to Salem with Channing in 1811, people were examining Swedenborgian theology, which rejected both the trinity and "inborn depravity, or original sin." Upon further study of Swedenborg's ideas, however, Elizabeth rejected his mysticism, which even her mother embraced. Mother and daughter eventually agreed not to discuss religion. And so "being herself" theologically started very young, and within her own family.[5]

In 1815, one of Channing's divinity students, John Emery Abbott, became the minister at North Church. Channing preached at his ordination, and told the Salem congregation that "True religion should be addressed at once to the understanding, and to the heart." Megan Marshall writes that Elizabeth "sought out" John Abbott after church on Sundays, "and won him over with intense questioning." Abbott's ministry was short-lived due to illness, unfortunately, but he had a lasting effect on Elizabeth—and, he let her use his personal library.[6]

When she was twelve, Elizabeth taught herself to read Hebrew to be able to read the Old Testament for herself. Borrowing books from Salem's circulating library, she also discovered the British Socinians, who put forth the idea that Christ was human, not divine. Even Unitarians found them extreme, and Elizabeth's mother was horrified to discover that her daughter's reading of the Socinians left her "with a feeling of strength in my mind, a sense of clearness in my ideas." As Megan Marshall explains, "reading the Socinians, Elizabeth found what seemed to her confirmation in both historical evidence and scriptural analysis of 'the literal humanity of Christ & the original freedom of man from total depravity.'"[7]

Elizabeth's parents ordered her to stop her reading, however. For one whole summer, she could only read the Bible. This she did. At the age of thirteen, Elizabeth read the New Testament thirty times in three months, examining and comparing points of doctrine and becoming even more convinced that her Unitarian ideas were right.

That summer, a Mrs. Davis, a friend of the family who was visiting Salem and who was a member of William

Ellery Channing's Federal Street Church in Boston, invited Elizabeth to stay with her for a while in Boston, to hear Channing preach, and to meet him. Elizabeth was enraptured when she did, and he was quite taken aback by her inquisitiveness and earnestness, by his own account. Channing taught her that "the religious life was one of constant education, development, and growth."[8]

When Elizabeth returned to Salem, she was staunchly Unitarian, in high spirits, and also determined to leave Salem, which she and her sisters, Mary and Sophia, found too confining and conservative. About Cambridge and Boston, she wrote, "you will not find any ladies there whose business is dressing and visiting—all have some serious purpose. [They] know that life is not given them to trifle away and while they would adorn and beautify it with everything beautiful in art or literature—they recollect that all these things are subservient to a higher aim." These were women who combined moral purpose with intellectual interests, and Elizabeth wanted to be among them.[9]

Elizabeth was bookish and serious. Bruce Ronda surmises that by the age of fifteen, she was wary of the prospects of marriage. "She could not fail to see that marriage and the demands of family life had effectively ended her mother's active intellectual life," he writes. "Although she would have male admirers in the next decade, and several displaced infatuations with utterly inappropriate men, Elizabeth could already discern that romance and marriage might result in the same stifled life. The stark choice that custom and culture presented to all women, and particularly to intellectual women, was clearly before her."[10]

In Elizabeth's family, it was the women who held intellectual and financial power. She could look at both sides of her family, the Palmers and Peabodys, and find men who were failures, seducers, or tyrants. Elizabeth had other things to do![11]

## Teaching

Elizabeth knew that teaching was her calling, despite the avenues traditionally closed off to female students and teachers. Before the 1780s, girls were excluded from town schools and if parents could afford some education for their daughters they sent them to a dame school, a local female academy, or a private tutor. But by the 1810s, some girls were entering town schools and by the 1820s, women were appearing in Massachusetts classrooms making this spectacle more commonplace.

Elizabeth began teaching school in 1820 in Lancaster, Massachusetts, where the family had moved to enable her father to try his hand at farming. It was "the vocation for which I had been educated from childhood," she wrote. It was not simply teaching a school, but educating children morally and spiritually as well as intellectually from the first; which my mother had taught me was the most sacred of the duties of the children of the Pilgrims, who founded the Republic to bless all the nations of the earth."[12]

She drew heavily on her mother's curriculum and teaching. In 1823, friends convinced Elizabeth to teach school in Hallowel, Maine, but she returned to the Boston area in 1825, at the age of twenty-one, to teach in Brookline where she was able to develop her friendship with William Ellery Channing. By this time, he had delivered perhaps his most important sermon in Baltimore, entitled *Unitarian Christianity*, in which he openly declared himself to be Unitarian and opened the door for other ministers to follow suit.

In Elizabeth, he had a faithful follower and friend. She became, in effect, his unpaid secretary. Oftentimes, their conversations, or intellectual investigations, became the subject of his sermons. That might have been acceptable to Channing's adult congregation, but in Elizabeth's school, when she attempted to engage her students in theological discussions, some parents became enraged. As Megan Marshall explains, "by suggesting that religion was a matter of inquiry rather than rote learning, Elizabeth had made a radical departure—even as she hoped to stimulate in her students the questioning frame of mind that she believed underlay all genuine learning."[13]

Channing helped her start a new school in Boston, and even enrolled his own daughter there. It was also at this time, when she was twenty-one, that Elizabeth wrote her spiritual autobiography. As I noted earlier, she was endlessly self-reflective, wanting to take measure of her interior life—where she was and what she had done.

She also began to write essays for publication, based on the conversations she was having with Channing. But unfortunately this is when their relationship soured. As she entered the public sphere, which women were still frowned upon for doing, Channing reminded her that her place was to be of service. It must have felt like a large dose of cold water.

## Transcendentalism and Kindergartens

At about this time, Elizabeth had been drawn to Transcendentalism as a way of thinking about individual development, our relationship to each other and the natural world, and the order of things. "Unitarianism," she wrote, "has a short mission in the world ... we should all survive it and find a new light."[14]

She became friends with Bronson Alcott, and taught at his Temple School in Boston. It was there that Elizabeth wrote her first original work, *Record of a School*, in which she not only promoted his school but also put forth her own ideas about early childhood education—that children were individuals whose unique gifts should be respected, nurtured, and enabled to grow. Published in 1835, Elizabeth's book is now considered among the first important works of Transcendentalism.

Elizabeth started spending time in Concord, Massachusetts, with Ralph Waldo Emerson, who had tutored her in Greek years earlier. She was teaching school, and developing her literary career. In Concord, she wrote, "I begin to grow independent," and it was during this time, thanks to Emerson's influence, that she determined to become more forceful in terms of her own internal power. "It was time," she resolved, "to be myself and act"... for in the end "the measure of our life is our power."[15]

She opened a bookstore and circulating library in Boston in 1840, which also served as a meeting place for Transcendentalists and was the site of the "Conversations" held by Margaret Fuller and other leading thinkers of their day.

Elizabeth became the first woman publisher in Boston, publishing works by Channing, Fuller, and her brother-in-law, Nathaniel Hawthorne.

She edited and published the *Dial*, the newspaper of the Transcendentalists.

And, in the late 1850s, Elizabeth encountered the ideas of Frederick Froebel on early childhood education. "Kindergarten," she wrote, "means a garden of children, and Froebel, the inventor of it, or rather as he would prefer to express it, the discoverer of the method of Nature, meant to symbolize by the name the spirit and plan of treatment. How does the gardener treat his plants? He studies their individual natures and puts them into such circumstances of soil and atmosphere as to enable them to grow, flower, and bring forth fruit … He does not expect to succeed unless he learns all their wants, and the circumstances in which these wants will be supplied, and all their possibilities of beauty and use, and the means of giving them the opportunity to be perfected."[16]

"A child is not a finite mass to be molded," she also wrote, "or a blank paper to be written upon at another's will. It is a living subject whose own cooperation—or at least willingness—is to be conciliated and made instrumental to the end in view."[17]

"Teachers often do great harm," she said, "with the best intentions … Encouragement to good should altogether predominate over warning and fault finding. It is often better, instead of blaming a child for short-coming, or even wrong doing, to pity and sympathize and, in a hopeful voice, speak of it as something which the child did not mean to do, or at least was sorry for as soon as done; suggesting at the same time, perhaps, how it can be avoided another time ... Let the teacher always appear as the friend who is saving or helping the child out of evil, rather than as the accuser, judge, or executioner."[18]

What impresses me is that Elizabeth Peabody came to this work in her early sixties. She referred to her years from ages sixty-one to sixty-three, when she traveled to Germany, as her "apprenticeship for life."

Indeed, Elizabeth served as a link between the visionaries of the Transcendentalist movement and the educational reforms that were taking place across the country. When she opened the first kindergarten in America in 1860, on Pinckney Street on Boston's Beacon Hill, the curriculum included arts, crafts, nature studies, science exploration, singing, dancing, conversation and reflection ... the emphasis was on children achieving success, learning through experimenting, appreciating nature, appreciating the individuality in themselves and all humans, and finding joy in working and playing together."[19]

Elizabeth also published a newspaper, the *Kindergarten Messenger*, and she organized the American Froebel Union.

As Bruce Ronda points out, kindergartens were her "Walden," or her "Nature" in the way that those great works of literature mark the legacies of Henry David Thoreau and Ralph Waldo Emerson. It was work she seemed born to do, and she did it well.[20]

Elizabeth Peabody died at the age of ninety, and she is buried in Concord, at Sleepy Hollow Cemetery with her Transcendentalist and literary friends. After a lifetime of hard work and self-reflection, I hope she was able to look back on her life and say, "Good for me. Well done" But I doubt it—she probably still had a long list of things she wanted to accomplish!

## Her Faith in Action

What strikes me about Elizabeth Peabody's faith journey, like others in this book, is her inquisitiveness and her refusal to accept any one doctrine at face value. Both of her parents had been tutors. Later, her mother taught school out of the family home and her father went on to become a some-time physician. Education, learning, and ideas were part of Elizabeth's family culture.

As Megan Marshall points out, Elizabeth was raised at a time when traditional Calvinist orthodoxy clashed with more progressive theology. At age seven, when she heard the Unitarian minister William Ellery Channing preach in Salem, it changed her life forever. Even at that young age, Elizabeth was trying to determine her own theology. Marshall writes that Elizabeth saw religion as "a subject of enquiry and dispute … not quite a settled thing that we must believe the popular system of theology" and that "true religion should be addressed at once to the understanding, and to the heart."[21]

Elizabeth's inquiring mind led her to study Hebrew to be able to read the Old Testament for herself. She investigated Swedenborgianism and the Socinians, rejecting some ideas but agreeing with others. As a result,

Elizabeth's parents insisted that she read only the Bible for one whole summer—which she did, thirty times. Soon after, as a teenager, she heard Channing preach again and thereafter was "staunchly Unitarian."

As a young teacher in Brookline, Massachusetts, Elizabeth tried to engage her young students in theological discussions. She suggested that religion was "a matter of inquiry rather than rote learning." But their parents would have none of it. At the same time, Elizabeth deepened her friendship with Channing and her commitment to Unitarianism by becoming his sort of secretary. Their conversations often turned up in his sermons. Now, at age twenty-one, she wrote her spiritual autobiography—acutely aware even then of her real-time spiritual journey.[22]

Elizabeth once wrote: "to contemplate the Spirit in ourselves, and in our fellow man, is obviously the only means of understanding social duty, and quickening within ourselves a wise Humanity—In general terms,— Contemplation of Spirit is the first principle of Human Culture; the foundation of Self-education."[23]

As one of her biographers, Joan Goodwin, explains: "In essence Elizabeth's own educational philosophy was a practical application of the Unitarian optimism as to the inherent human goodness, especially of the young, combined with the ideas of self-culture she took from Channing. She had always taught by foregrounding her own intellectual delight and curiosity as the means of inspiring children both to enjoy learning and also to take on greater moral responsibility. "When a child has been led to enjoy his intellectual life, in any way," she wrote, "and then is made to observe whence his enjoyment has arisen, he can feel and understand the argument of duty which may be urged in favor of attention."[24]

Elizabeth parted ways with Channing to pursue her own interests and that included Transcendentalism. "Unitarianism," she wrote, "has a short mission in the world ... we should all survive it and find a new light." She became friends with Bronson Alcott, putting their shared "faith in action" principles to work at his Temple School in Boston. As in Nature, they believed, children were unique buds who needed to be respected, nurtured, and enabled to grow fully into who they were meant to be.[25]

At her bookstore in Boston, Elizabeth published the Transcendentalist newspaper the *Dial*, hosted Margaret Fuller's "Conversations" for women, and encouraged intellectual and spiritual pursuit through her lending library. But it was when she encountered the teachings of Frederick Froebel on early childhood education that her spiritual self really swung into action. To repeat this quote from her:

"Kindergarten," Elizabeth wrote, "means a garden of children, and Froebel, the inventor of it, or rather as he would prefer to express it, the discoverer of the method of Nature, meant to symbolize by the name the spirit and plan of treatment. How does the gardener treat his plants? He studies their individual natures and puts them into such circumstances of soil and atmosphere as to enable them to grow, flower, and bring forth fruit ... He does not expect to succeed unless he learns all their wants, and the circumstances in which these wants will be supplied, and all their possibilities of beauty and use, and the means of giving them the opportunity to be perfected."[26]

Today, we take it for granted that this is how children should be treated. But it was Elizabeth Peabody's faith in action that really started the United States down this path. Toward the end of her life, Elizabeth's faith in action, along with her sister Mary's, extended to woman suffrage, Native American rights, and world peace.

**Sites to Visit**

Home of Elizabeth Peabody
Brown Building
Corner of Union and Essex Streets
Salem, MA 01970
*Elizabeth's family lived here in 1810, and possibly earlier.*

Home of Elizabeth Peabody
54 Charter Street
Salem, MA 01970
*Elizabeth's family moved here in 1835.*

Home and Bookstore of Elizabeth Peabody
15 West Street
Boston, MA 02111
*Elizabeth lived and worked here starting in 1840; this is where Margaret Fuller held her "Conversations."*

Temple School (site of)
Masonic Temple
Corner of Tremont Street and Temple Place
Boston, MA 02111
*Elizabeth taught school here from 1834 to 1835.*

Federal Street Church (site of)
Corner of Franklin and Federal Streets
Boston, MA 02111
*Like many of her Transcendentalist friends, Elizabeth attended this church led by William Ellery Channing and she served as his some-time secretary. A plaque marks the spot.*

First Kindergarten in America (site of)
15 Pinckney Street
Boston, MA 02108
*Elizabeth opened this school in 1861. The building no longer stands, but it was the mirror image of 17 Pinckney Street.*

Home of Ralph Waldo Emerson
28 Cambridge Turnpike
Concord, MA 01742
*Elizabeth was a frequent guest in this house.*

Gravesite of Elizabeth Peabody
Sleepy Hollow Cemetery
Bedford Street
Concord, MA 01742
*Follow the signs to Author's Ridge.*

## Resources

*Elizabeth Peabody: A Reformer on Her Own Terms* by Bruce Ronda (Harvard University Press, 1999).

*The Peabody Sisters of Salem: Three Women Who Ignited American Romanticism* by Megan Marshall (Houghton Mifflin, 2005).

*Standing Before Us: Unitarian and Universalist Women and Social Reform, 1776-1936* by Dorothy May Emerson (Skinner House, 2000).

Websites:
*Search for Elizabeth Peabody at:*
Boston Women's Heritage Trail
Dictionary of Unitarian Universalist Biography
Salem Women's Heritage Trail

## Notes to the Biographical Sketch

1   *Elizabeth Peabody: A Reformer on Her Own Terms* by Bruce Ronda (Harvard University Press, 1999), 3.
2   Ibid., 8.
3   Ibid., 44.
4   *The Peabody Sisters of Salem: Three Women Who Ignited American Romanticism* by Megan Marshall (Houghton Mifflin, 2005), 7.
5   Marshall, 7.
6   Ibid., 8.
7   Ibid., 9.
8   Ronda, 66.
9   Ibid., 52.
10   Ibid., 48.
11   Ibid., 76.
12   Ibid., 50.
13   Marshall, 14.
14   *Standing Before Us* by Dorothy May Emerson, ed. (Skinner House, 2000).
15   Marshall, 17.
16   Emerson.
17   Emerson, 219.
18   Ibid., 219-20.
19   Emerson, 223.
20   Ronda.
21   Marshall, 7-8.
22   Marshall, 14.
23   "Elizabeth Peabody" by Joan Goodwin for the *Dictionary of Unitarian Universalist Biography*.
24   Ibid.
25   Emerson.
26   Emerson.

"I thought of the great injustice practiced upon me, and longed for some power to help me crush those who thus robbed me of my personal rights.

I appeal on behalf of four millions of men, women, and children who are chattels in the Southern States of America, Not because they are identical with my race and color, though I am proud of that identity, but because they are men and women. The sum of sixteen hundred millions of dollars is invested in their bones, sinews, and flesh—is this not sufficient reason why all the friends of humanity should not endeavor with all their might and power, to overturn the vile systems of slavery."

*—Sarah Parker Remond*

# Sarah Parker Remond

## (1814–1894)

### Her Achievements

* Most famous African American female anti-slavery speaker at a time when public speaking for women was new
* As a speaker, highly successful fundraiser for the American Anti-Slavery Society
* Spoke in Europe before audiences who had never seen an African American woman
* Spoke in America before mixed race audiences, which was a new phenomenon
* Broke barriers for women by playing a leadership role in anti-slavery societies

*(more)*

- Committed an act of civil disobedience that led to a large financial settlement, national attention, and a desegregated theater in Boston
- Fundraiser and organizer of freedmen's aid societies
- Co-founder of the London Ladies Emancipation Society
- Studied and practiced medicine in Italy

**Her Story**

When Sarah Parker Remond took to the stage to speak out against slavery, people listened. She called for an immediate end to slavery, not the gradual dissolution some people advocated. She appealed especially to women, pointing out the "sufferings and indignities" endured by enslaved women at the hands of their masters, the destruction of families, and the "sinfulness" that affected blacks and whites alike. She urged Americans not to allow a small handful of slave owners dominate national policy, and she challenged Europeans to end their reliance on Southern cotton.[1]

Born in 1824 or 1826 (there are conflicting records), Sarah was raised in a prominent African American abolitionist family in Salem, Massachusetts, as the seventh of eight children. Her father, John Remond (altered from "Vonreman" and pronounced "REH-mond"), hailed from Curaçao in the West Indies and became a successful caterer and hair salon owner after arriving in America, alone, at age ten. Sarah's mother, Nancy Lenox Remond, the daughter of a Revolutionary War veteran, had been born free in Newton, Massachusetts, and worked with her husband as a "fancy baker." As one historian described her, Nancy Remond raised her children to be "prepared, aware, able to cope with racism, and filled with self-esteem."[2]

As a girl, Sarah and her siblings attended Salem's (then) integrated schools, adopting the Remond family's strong emphasis on education. Unfortunately, when she and her sister placed well in Salem High School's entrance exam, they were turned away because of their race. Sarah retained early childhood memories of "deep rooted, hateful, cruel prejudice."[3]

Because of the treatment his daughters received, John Remond moved his family to Newport, Rhode Island, where the children attended an all-black private school. Meanwhile, he worked to desegregate Salem's schools, and by 1841 he succeeded. The Remonds returned to Salem, and their home once again became a haven for abolitionists, both black and white, and for fugitive slaves.[4]

Sarah continued to read books, plays, and poems, to attend lectures and concerts, and really embrace her "independent education." In her autobiography, written many years later, Sarah explained, "My strongest desire through life has been to be educated. I found the most exquisite pleasure in reading, and as we had no library, I read every book which came in my way, and I longed for more. Again and again mother would endeavor to have us placed in some private school, but being colored we were refused."[5]

## Abolition

By 1841, Sarah's older brother, Charles Lenox Remond, had become the president of the Massachusetts Anti-

Slavery Society and a popular public speaker. Earlier, Angelina and Sarah Grimké had initiated their anti-slavery tour through New England paving the way for more women to speak publicly. Sarah joined the interracial Salem Female Anti-Slavery Society in 1841, and the following year she gave her first speech. Sarah Remond spent the next decade speaking, raising money, and organizing for the cause including before mixed race audiences, which was a new phenomenon.

Other anti-slavery societies thrived as well. William Lloyd Garrison had founded the New England Anti-Slavery Society in 1831 and its newspaper, the *Liberator*. In 1833, he started the American Anti-Slavery Society, which Charles Remond spoke for until Frederick Douglass, the escaped slave, replaced him in 1842 as the society's leading speaker. All of their work took on new meaning in 1850 when the U. S. Congress passed the Fugitive Slave Act, making it illegal for anyone in the North to knowingly harbor or help escaped slaves and not return them to their "owners" in the South.[6]

Many years later, in her short autobiography, Sarah wrote:

"Previous to the year 1829, no decided effort had been made in behalf of the slave population. Now, a young man, a native of the state of Massachusetts, essentially a man of the people, demands the immediate emancipation of every slave as the right of the victim and the duty of the master. His clarion voice is heard, and the nation wonders. What? The negro a man! The American people had never dreamed that the slaves had rights in common with themselves and a demand based upon justice filled the people with consternation! They considered the colored race as so many beasts of burthen. My mother hailed the advent of this young and noble apostle of liberty with enthusiasm, and among my earliest impressions is mingled the name of that now venerated friend of the oppressed, William L. Garrison.

As years rolled by, I became more and more interested in every effort made in behalf of the enslaved. The germ of a glorious reform was now planted, and had taken root; the American anti-slavery society was founded, based upon principles which in every age had broken the bonds of the oppressor and elevated humanity. Auxiliary societies were formed in different localities of the free states, and a nucleus formed, around which the friends of freedom have rallied. Although mobocracy and various kinds of persecution met them on every hand, all who had counted the cost, and were in earnest, still pursued their way, trusting in the justice of their cause.

My eldest brother, early in the conflict, publicly advocated the cause of his enslaved countrymen, and from my earliest days, until I left the States, fifteen months since, I have attended the public meetings of the abolitionists. I am grateful beyond expression for the many influences which led me to become familiar with the principles and mode of action destined to completely upset that vile system of American chattel slavery, which is, at the present time, demoralising the various ramifications of the country."[7]

The other momentous act of legislation passed by Congress in 1850 was the Compromise of 1850, which expanded slavery in some territories while restricting its expansion elsewhere. Tensions around the issues of slavery, racism, and segregation were at fever pitch.

In 1853, at the age of twenty-seven, Sarah committed her first act of public resistance in Boston. She had purchased tickets by courier to see the opera *Don Pasquale* at the Howard Athenaeum. When Sarah and her sister, Caroline, and their friend, the abolitionist William Cooper Nell, arrived to see the performance, they were shown to the segregated section. Sarah refused to go. A policeman attempted to remove her physically, injuring her shoulder and tearing her dress in the process. Sarah sued the theater, and won $500. Her case received national attention. She had truly struck a blow against segregated facilities; the theater was forced to integrate its seating.[8]

### Speaking

Sarah's activism continued, and in 1856 the American Anti-Slavery Society engaged her for a lengthy speaking tour across the country. According to the National Women's History Museum, she was treated with less hostility the further west she traveled. What's more, she traveled without a male escort, which was highly unusual at the time. In her autobiography Sarah wrote, "Upon the obstacles which met with me after this determination I do not think it necessary to dwell. I was quite determined to persevere."[9]

In 1857, encouraged by the abolitionist and feminist Abby Kelly Foster, Sarah joined her brother, Charles, and a group of white abolitionists for a speaking tour in New York on behalf of the American Anti-Slavery Society. That same year, the Dred Scott Decision denied citizenship to African American men and the *Freedman*, a newspaper in

London, published Sarah's speech "The Freeman or the Emancipated Negro of the Southern States of the United States." By the end of that year, Sarah had achieved considerable fame.

Sarah was well aware of the barriers she was breaking down as both an African American and a woman, and in 1858 Sarah joined Susan B. Anthony and other women leaders as a speaker for the annual Women's Rights Convention held that year in New York State.

That fall, Sarah made a momentous decision when she agreed to travel to Liverpool, England, on a speaking tour for the American Anti-Slavery Society. As Marilyn Richardson explains her decision:

"Historian Karen Jean Hunt identifies three goals that anti-slavery lecturer Sarah Parker Remond had in mind when she first sailed from Boston for Liverpool in September of 1858. One was to remove herself from the daily toxicity of American racism. Another was to do all she could to consolidate anti-slavery sentiment on the eve of the Civil War by arguing the ethical and economic advantages of British support for the Union during the War. The third was to secure for herself an education superior to any available to her at home."[10]

Sarah delivered her first speech on January 24, 1859. On March 11, William Lloyd Garrison gave her front-page coverage in the *Liberator*. Other American newspapers followed her success as well. Between 1859 and 1861, Sarah presented at least forty-five lectures in England, Ireland, and Scotland. As one biographer notes, "Her speaking schedule, before groups of up to two thousand strong, kept her on the road and often near exhaustion." William Lloyd Garrison praised Sarah's "calm, dignified manner, her winning personal appearance, and her earnest appeals to the conscience and heart."[11]

In a speech Sarah delivered (without notes) in Liverpool in 1859, she stated:

"I appeal on behalf of four millions of men, women, and children who are chattels in the Southern States of America, Not because they are identical with my race and color, though I am proud of that identity, but because they are men and women. The sum of sixteen hundred millions of dollars is invested in their bones, sinews, and flesh—is this not sufficient reason why all the friends of humanity should not endeavor with all their might and power, to overturn the vile system of slavery."[12]

The *Anti-Slavery Advocate* wrote about her speech:

"Miss Remond was most cordially received, and proceeded with a calmness of manner, which was all the more striking from her evident depth of feeling and earnestness of purpose, to lay before her auditors the wrongs of her race, the iniquitous laws under which the coloured people are placed, and the oppression they suffer in the United States …

She spoke for an hour with the utmost readiness and clearness, with an admirable choice of words, and with a womanly dignity, which were the admiration of all who heard her. Most touching and forcible were her representations and appeals with respect to the apathy and guilty connivance of the Churches of America in relation to the sin of slavery, and their shameful treatment, even in their places of worship, of the coloured race."[13]

Sarah wrote to Maria Weston Chapman in Boston, a founder of the Boston Female Anti-Slavery Society, "I shall on every occasion that I can still continue to lecture and do all I can for our cause. I have lectured very frequently, in fact had more invitations recently than I could fill. Lectured on three successive evenings last week which was rather too much for me and I am now with my friends Mr & Mrs Robson for a little rest, then go to York, to lecture there."[14]

Sarah struck another blow in 1859 when the American legation in London denied her permission to travel to France because of her political activities and because legally, as an African American, under the Dred Scott Decision, they did not consider her an American citizen. She fought their decision, and won.

Also in 1859, John Brown and a group of his followers raided the federal armory at Harper's Ferry. They planned to lead a slave uprising in the South, arming African American men with the means to free themselves and their families. Many Northerners supported John Brown and his belief that only through violent means would slavery end. But Brown was caught, captured, and hanged. In England, the *Leeds Mercury* described a speech Sarah gave about John Brown's death:

"To her, that was a solemn and a sad hour. Every letter she received from across the Atlantic brought her tidings of the excitement rocking that land from its centre to its circumference, and she was constantly told—'Old John Brown sleeps to night in a martyr's grave.' She had no word of censure for him, or for the means which he took to carry out his great idea …

What was the condition of America, enfolding within her warmest sympathies and encircling by her strong influence a system so foul and hideous that it called forth the execrations of the civilised world? Turn where they would, whether they regarded the legislative, the executive, the judicial, the political, or the religious opinions of that land, they found that, so far as the majority was concerned, they were wedded to slavery …

American politics had sunk to a depth of degradation which she could not describe, and all the best men in America, with few exceptions, were outside the political arena. Even the Republican party had never dared to go beyond seeking to prevent the extension of slavery, and they had not yet laid the axe at the root of the tree …

Every word of sympathy from English lips would tell in favour of the slave, and she asked them to send their moral protest across the Atlantic against the oligarchy which was crushing her brethren and sisters and reducing them to the lowest degradation. She referred to the support given to slavery by the religious and moral sentiment of America, and asserted that if this sentiment were really and truly opposed to slavery that curse would go down at once."[15]

## College

Meanwhile, in 1860, Sarah was attending lectures at the "Ladies College" in London (Bedford College, today part of the University of London) and decided to pursue the higher education that had been denied her in the United States. "Prejudice against color has always been the one thing, above all others, which has cast its gigantic shadow over my whole life," she wrote in her autobiography. Sarah enrolled at Bedford College where she studied biblical literature, moral philosophy, ancient and modern history, mathematics, natural philosophy, geography, languages, music, and elocution. The following year, 1861, *The English Women's Journal* published an excerpt from Sarah's autobiography, "A Colored Lady Lecturer."[16]

## War

In America, war broke out in 1861, the year following President Abraham Lincoln's election, when Confederate troops attacked the federal Fort Sumter. English businessmen paid close attention as their leading industry, textile production, relied on Southern cotton. Sarah continued to lecture and raise funds, and in 1864, the year after President Lincoln signed the Emancipation Proclamation, Sarah helped to establish the London Ladies Emancipation Society, which "supported causes beyond the abolition of slavery in the United States." She also worked with the British Freedmen's Aid Society, and returned briefly to America in 1865 after the war. She spoke in New York on behalf of the American Equal Rights Association along with her brother, Charles, and Frederick Douglass, but she returned to England in 1867 to study nursing.[17]

As a transplanted Londoner, Sarah had already visited Italy several times. Her reformer friends in England had introduced her to revolutionaries from that country, including Giuseppe Mazzini, whose efforts to unify Italy

Margaret Fuller had also supported, and Giuseppe Garibaldi, the leading figure of the Italian Revolution. Sarah "had her eye on Italy," specifically, Florence.[18]

**Italy**

At age forty, Sarah's Italian adventure began. She enrolled at the Santa Maria Nuova Hospital in Florence to study medicine, graduating in 1871, and for the next twenty years worked as a practicing physician. The (black) *Christian Recorder* noted: "Miss Sarah Remond, a gifted colored lady, who studied medicine with Dr. Appleton—the friend and physician of [abolitionist] Theodore Parker, during the latter portion of his life at Rome and Florence, has been regularly admitted as a practitioner of midwifery in Florence, where she is now residing, with excellent prospects of employment and success. Her merit has won her friends on the continent of Europe, as it did in England."[19]

Six years later, in 1877, at the age of fifty-three, Sarah married Lazzaro Pintor of Sardinia. Very little is known about their marriage, unfortunately, or about Sarah's final days, but as one historian notes:

"She was in her fifties when they wed in Florence, and she was on her own in Rome within three years ... In any event, the woman who is identified in history books and commemorated in memorials as Sarah Parker Remond lived and died in Rome as Signora Pintor. She is listed in burial records at the Non-Catholic Cemetery (Cimitero Prostestante) there as Sara [sic] Remond Pintor."[20]

Starting in 2011, an effort has been underway to install a

plaque in Sarah's memory at the Non-Catholic Cemetery.

## Her Faith in Action

It is unclear how Sarah was raised religiously in Salem, but she certainly referred to Christian ideals when she gave her anti-slavery speeches. She urged Christians to exert their moral influence and end the evil institution of slavery. She believed God had created everyone equally, and that the law of God was supreme. She chastised ministers for their support of slavery, or for their apathy, and urged them to lead the way toward complete and immediate abolition.

About her 1859 speech delivered in Liverpool, England, the *Anti-Slavery Advocate* wrote:

"She spoke for an hour with the utmost readiness and clearness, with an admirable choice of words, and with a womanly dignity, which were the admiration of all who heard her. Most touching and forcible were her representations and appeals with respect to the apathy and guilty connivance of the Churches of America in relation to the sin of slavery, and their shameful treatment, even in their places of worship, of the coloured race …

There was no excitement in her tone, no exaggeration in her language; but she reached the understandings and the hearts of those before her the more effectually on this account, and made every one feel the enormity of the wickedness she was exposing. 'Shame, shame!' was frequently on the lips of her audience, as she set forth the lack of faithfulness in the anti-slavery cause manifested by religious parties in her country; and no right-minded person could resist the conviction that they are verily guilty concerning their coloured brethren."[21]

The *Leeds Mercury's* account of her speech about John Brown's hanging included these words:

"Every word of sympathy from English lips would tell in favour of the slave, and she asked them to send their moral protest across the Atlantic against the oligarchy which was crushing her brethren and sisters and reducing them to the lowest degradation. She referred to the support given to slavery by the religious and moral sentiment of America, and asserted that if this sentiment were really and truly opposed to slavery that curse would go down at once …

The clergymen of the States did more to carry out the fugitive slave law than any other portion of the community, and as a body they had much to answer for in this respect. Miss Remond concluded by an eloquent tribute to the memory of John Brown."[22]

### Sites to Visit in Massachusetts

Home of Sarah Parker Remond (site of)
9 Dean Street (today, the part of Flint Street that runs between Essex and Federal Streets)
Salem, MA 01970
*This is the site of Sarah's childhood home.*

Hamilton Hall
9 Chestnut Street
Salem, MA 01970
*Site of John Remond's successful catering business.*

Harmony Grove Cemetery
30 Grove Street
Salem, MA 01970
*Sarah's parents, her brother Charles, and some of her
other siblings are buried here.*

Howard Athenaeum (site of)
Scollay Square
Government Center
Boston, MA 02108
*This is where Sarah committed her first act of public
resistance.*

State House Women's Leadership Project
Massachusetts State House
Beacon Street
Boston, MA 02108
*Sarah is one of six women featured in this text-and-image
sculpture on the second floor, outside Doric Hall.*

## Resources

"A Colored Lady Lecturer" in *The English Woman's
Journal*, vol. 7 (June, 1861).

"An Historic Legacy Revealed" by Abaigeal Duda in *PEM
Connections* (January/February, 2006).

"Sarah Parker Remond: Black Abolitionist from Salem" by
Ruth Bogin in *Essex Institute Historical Collections* #110
(April 1974).

"The Remonds of Salem, Massachusetts: A Nineteenth-
Century Family Revisited" by Dorothy Burnett Porter

Wesley in *Proceedings of the American Antiquarian Society* (October, 1985).

*African American Heritage Sites in Salem, Massachusetts* by Rae Emerson (Salem Maritime National Historic Site, 1998, available at www.nps.gov/sama).

*Black Women Abolitionists: A Study of Activism, 1828-1860* by Shirley J. Yee (University of Tennessee Press, 1992).

*Building an Antislavery Wall: Black Americans in the Atlantic Abolitionist Movement, 1830-1860* by R.J.M. Blackett (Louisiana State University Press, 1983).

Websites
*Search for Sarah Parker Remond at:*
Sarah Parker Remond Wordpress Blog
    *Maintained by the historian Marilyn Richardson, this site contains the most recent and accurate information about Sarah.*
Boston Women's Heritage Trail
Civil War Women Blog
MassHumanities

## Notes to the Biographical Sketch

1    See http://sarahparkerremond.wordpress.com. (hereafter referred to as "SPR Blog").
2    SPR Blog, "An Historic Legacy Revealed" by Abaigeal Duda in *PEM Connections*, Jan/Feb 2006, and presentation by Merrill Kohlhoffer at the Salem Maritime National Historic Site in Salem, Massachusetts, February 14, 2010.
3    SPR Blog, and Kohlhoffer.
4    Finding Aid, Remond Papers, Peabody Essex Museum, Salem, Massachusetts.

5   "Sarah Parker Remond" on National Women's History Museum website, and "State House Women's Leadership Project" of Mass Humanities.
6   I put the word "owners" in quotes because there really is no such thing ethically and morally as one human being owning another.
7   "A Colored Lady Lecturer" by Sarah Parker Remond in *The English Woman's Journal*, vol. 7, June, 1861.
8   SPR Blog.
9   Remond.
10  SPR Blog.
11  SPR Blog, and http://www.masshumanities.org/shwlp honorees/remond.html.
12  SPR speech, published on SPR Blog.
13  *Anti-Slavery Advocate*, October 1859, published on SPR Blog.
14  SPR Blog.
15  *Leeds Mercury*, 24 December 1859, published on SPR Blog.
16  SPR Blog, and http://www.civilwarwomenblog com/2006/11/sarah-parker-remond.html.
17  SPR Blog.
18  SPR Blog.
19  *Christian Recorder*, published on SPR Blog.
20  SPR Blog.
21  *Anti-Slavery Advocate*, October 1859, published on SPR Blog.
22  *Leeds Mercury*, 24 December 1859, published on SPR Blog.

"Prejudice against colour has always been the one thing, above all others, which has cast its gigantic shadow over my whole life."

—*Sarah Parker Remond*

"I felt that I had a great work to perform; and was in haste to make a profession of my faith in Christ, that I might be about my Father's business. Soon after I made this profession, The Spirit of God came before me, and I spake before many … A something said within my breast, 'Press forward, I will be with thee.

"And my heart made this reply, 'Lord, if thou wilt be with me, then I will speak for thee as long as I live.' And thus far I have every reason to believe that it is the divine influence of the Holy Spirit operating upon my heart that could possibly induce me to make the feeble and unworthy efforts that I have."

—*Maria Miller Stewart*

# Maria Miller Stewart

## (1803–1879)

---

### Her Achievements

- First American-born female public speaker
- First woman to speak in public before a "promiscuous" audience, meaning, men and women
- First American woman to lecture on political themes
- First African American woman political writer
- Probably the first African American to lecture in defense of women's rights
- "Forerunner to generations of the best known and most influential champions of black activism, both male and female"[1]
- Journalist

*(more)*

---

- Author
- Teacher and Vice Principal
- School Founder
- Matron of a Hospital for Freedmen

## Her Story

Maria Stewart was the first American-born woman to speak on a public stage. And she was the first African American woman. The courage she displayed on behalf of African Americans and women and the risks she took with her physical safety, reputation, and social standing, leave me completely in awe. But she did it. She also wrote compelling anti-slavery and anti-racism articles, taught school, and ran a hospital for freed slaves after the Civil War.

She truly embodied faith in action. After a religious conversation, the two were inseparable.

Maria Stewart was born in 1803 as Maria Miller in Hartford, Connecticut. The names and occupations of her parents are unknown, but they both died when she was five years old. Maria was then hired out as a servant in the household of a minister until she was fifteen. She experienced hard work and drudgery first-hand, but she also read books in the minister's library and lived in a deeply religious family culture.

When Maria left the minister's household, she appears to have supported herself as a domestic servant. According to the historian Marilyn Richardson, Maria "struggled to gather isolated fragments of an education when and where she could, attending Sabbath school classes which offered the rudiments of literacy along with religious instruction."[2]

Maria came of age at a time of racial political unrest in other parts of the world, like Haiti, where a violent slave uprising had taken place. White people in Boston were aware of such events, and fearfully and with suspicion kept the city's neighborhoods and occupations segregated.

When Maria married James W. Stewart in 1826, assuming his middle initial and last name (at his request), they settled in Boston on the segregated back side of Beacon Hill. They were married by the Reverend Thomas Paul, the founding minister of Boston's African Baptist Church, in the African Meeting House which was the center of political, religious, and cultural thought and activity for Boston's black community. Anti-slavery society meetings took place there, and a school welcomed African American children.[3]

Maria was twenty-three at the time of her marriage. James was a Navy veteran of the War of 1812. He had been held prisoner during the war, but now he was a successful shipping agent and businessman with an office on Broad Street. The couple quickly became fixtures of Boston's black middle class community but, sadly, the marriage only lasted three years. James died suddenly in 1829. The money he left his wife was confiscated by the white executors of his estate, leaving Maria with nothing.

## Abolition

Six months after James died, a man named David Walker

also died. Maria had met this inspiring anti-slavery leader several years earlier and she had been moved by his courageous book *An Appeal, In Four Articles; Together with a Preamble, To the Coloured Citizens Of The World, But in Particular, And Very Expressly, To Those Of The United States Of America.* David Walker owned a clothing shop on Brattle Street in Boston, and it is thought that he smuggled copies of his book onboard ships heading South that he and James Stewart helped provision.

Historian Henry Highland Garnet, who wrote about the *Appeal* in 1848, stated, "This little book produced more commotion amongst slaveholders than any volume of its size that was ever issued from an American press." David Walker also contributed to the first black newspaper, *Freedom's Journal*, and served as its agent in Boston.[4]

The four themes in David Walker's book included "wretchedness" in consequence of slavery, ignorance, Christian ministers, and the colonization scheme he was dead set against. Walker was very religious and a Christian. His writings were filled with Biblical references and themes. He condemned the hypocrisy of the ministers who supported slavery. He counseled African Americans to view education as the answer to blacks advancing in life and proving their abilities. Marilyn Richardson points out that he was Maria's "political and intellectual mentor."[5]

How David Walker died remains a mystery. A group of slave owners in Georgia had offered a large reward for him to be killed or captured. At the time, David was urged to leave Boston for Canada but he chose to stand his ground. It is possible he was poisoned to death in 1830, but we will probably never know.

## Conversion

After the deaths of the two most important men in her life, Maria went through a religious conversion in which she became convinced that God was calling her to become a "warrior for God and for freedom." As she explained:

"From the moment I experienced the change I felt a strong desire … to devote the remainder of my days to piety and virtue and now possess that spirit of independence that, were I called upon, I would willingly sacrifice my life for the cause of God and my brethren. All the nations of the earth are crying out for liberty and equality. Away, away with tyranny and oppression! And shall Afric's sons be silent any longer? … Many will suffer for pleading the cause of oppressed Africa, and I shall glory in being one of her martyrs … [God] is able to take me to himself, as he did the most noble, fearless, and undaunted David Walker."[6]

## Voice

In 1831, Nat Turner's slave rebellion in Virginia, his death and those of hundreds more slaves, fueled Maria's resolve. In the same year, William Lloyd Garrison founded the New England Anti-Slavery Society and began to publish his newspaper the *Liberator*. Maria met Garrison at his Boston office and the two formed a real partnership. From then on, he published almost everything Maria wrote. At the close of 1831, he had published her first essay "Religion and the Pure Principles of Morality: The Sure Foundation on Which We Must Build" in the *Liberator* and then as a pamphlet. Maria used her own name, thus assuming a literary and political authority usually relegated only to men.

And then, in September of 1832, Maria Stewart "did what no American-born woman, black or white, before her is recorded as having done," Marilyn Richardson writes. "She mounted a lecture platform and raised a political argument before a 'promiscuous' audience, that is, one composed of both men and women." In her speech Maria spoke out against the colonization movement, which would have African Americans returned to Africa to establish a colony in Liberia. Instead, Maria and others argued, they were Americans with just as much right to live and thrive in their home land having helped build the country.[7]

Between 1832 and 1833, Maria Stewart delivered four public lectures for the African American Female Intelligence Society of Boston. Garrison published her speeches in the *Liberator*. Maria had mastered public speaking, displayed impressive rhetorical power, and used the full force of her religious conviction. When she was criticized for putting herself forward, as a woman, she defended herself by arguing that she was an instrument in God's hands. Maria would not have her voice be silenced, nor that of any other woman. As she put it:

"What if I am a woman; is not the God of ancient times the God of these modern days? Did he not raise up Deborah, to be a mother, and a judge in Israel? Did not Queen Esther save the lives of the Jews? And Mary Magdalene first declared the resurrection of Christ from the dead? ... If such women as are here described have once existed, be no longer astonished ... that God ... should raise up your own females."[8]

That voice was heard again in 1832 when Maria published

her pamphlet *Meditations from the Pen of Mrs. Maria Stewart*. But she was becoming politically unpopular in Boston, and Maria decided to move to New York in 1834 to teach school.

Like her mentor, David Walker, Maria believed strongly in the transformative power of education. She "encouraged [African Americans] to plan wisely for their future in this country, to see to the establishment of strong, self-sufficient educational and economic institutions within their own community," Marilyn Richardson writes.[9]

For African American women, she "dreamed of the day when black women could build their own high school, that the higher branches of knowledge might be enjoyed by us." And, famously, she asked, "How long shall the fair daughters of Africa be compelled to bury their minds and talents beneath a load of iron pots and kettles?" Reflecting on great women in ancient history, she wrote, "What if such women as are here described should rise among our sable race? And it is not impossible. For it is not the color of the skin that makes the man or the woman, but the principle formed in the soul. Brilliant wit will shine, come from whence it will; and genius and talent will not hide the brightness of its luster."[10]

On September 21, 1833, before departing for New York Maria Stewart delivered a farewell address to members and friends of the Belknap Street Church (African Meeting House). Looking back on her Boston years, she wrote:

"On my arrival here, not finding scarce an individual who felt interested in these subjects [putting faith into action], and but few whites, except Mr. Garrison, and his friend, Mr. Knapp; and hearing that those gentlemen had observed that female influence was powerful, my soul became fired with a holy zeal for your cause; every nerve and muscle in me was engaged in your behalf. I felt that I had a great work to perform; and was in haste to make a profession of my faith in Christ, that I might be about my Father's business. Soon after I made this profession, the Spirit of God came before me, and I spake before many … A something said within my breast, 'Press forward, I will be with thee.' And my heart made this reply, Lord, if thou wilt be with me, then I will speak for thee as long as I live. And thus far I have every reason to believe that it is the divine influence of the Holy Spirit operating upon my heart that could possibly induce me to make the feeble and unworthy efforts that I have."[11]

She continued:

"The mighty work of reformation has begun … The dark clouds of ignorance are dispersing. The light of science is bursting forth. Knowledge is beginning to flow, nor will its moral influence be extinguished till its refulgent rays have spread over us from East to West, and from North to South. Thus far is this mighty work begun, but not as yet accomplished. Christians must awake from their slumbers. Religion must flourish among them before the church will be built up in its purity, or immortality be suppressed …

Yet notwithstanding your prospects are thus fair and bright, I am about to leave you, perhaps never more to return. For I find it is no use for me as an individual to try to make myself useful among my color in this city. It was contempt for my moral and religious opinions in private that drove me thus before the public. Had experience more plainly shown me that it was the nature of man to crush his fellow, I should not have thought it so hard. Wherefore, my respected friends, let us no longer talk of prejudice, till prejudice becomes extinct at home. Let us no longer talk of opposition, till we cease to oppose our own. For while these evils exist, to talk is like giving breath to the air, and labor to the wind."[12]

With that, Maria Stewart left for New York, where she taught at the Williamsburg "colored school" and at schools in Manhattan and Brooklyn. In 1835, the "Friends of Freedom and Virtue" in Boston published her book *Productions of Mrs. Maria W. Stewart*. She attended the Women's Anti-Slavery Convention in New York in 1837, and was appointed assistant to the principal at the Williamsburg school that year. Then, she moved to Baltimore in 1852 or 1853 to teach privately, and, finally, to Washington, D.C. in 1861.[13]

In the early 1870s, while continuing to teach, Maria was appointed Matron of the Freedmen's Hospital in Washington, D.C. (today, Howard University Hospital) most of whose patients were former slaves. She also started a Sunday school in her neighborhood. Then, in 1878, as a result of changes in federal legislation, Maria became eligible to claim a pension as the widow of a veteran. She received this money in 1879, and decided to reissue her book under the title *Meditations From The Pen of Mrs. Maria Stewart*. This edition included letters and commendations praising the first edition, which, as Marilyn Richardson points out, was reminiscent of the time when other African American writers, like Phillis Wheatley, needed prominent whites to vouch for "both their character and ability."[14]

Later that year, 1879, Maria Stewart died at the Freedmen's Hospital and was buried in Washington, D.C.'s integrated Graceland Cemetery (today, Woodlawn Cemetery). She was seventy-six years old.

## Her Faith in Action

If she were alive today, Maria Stewart would surely be an ordained minister with a national ministry and international influence.

As a child, living as a servant in the household of a minister, she heard and read Christian theology. But it was her conversion experience, after the deaths of her husband, James, and David Walker that turned her into an agent of the will of God—a warrior in the fight to end slavery. As Marilyn Richardson writes, it would be inappropriate "to separate [her] secular documents from the pervasive religious consciousness which informs her analyses. Stewart's intense piety shaped her decidedly evangelical style. Her incorporation into her texts of numerous biblical passages, occasional stanzas from hymns, and, at one point, a forthright invitation to prayer, was commonplace to the audiences she addressed. Her belief and theirs was that God and humanity must work in concert toward the day when 'knowledge would begin to flow, and the chains of slavery and ignorance would melt like wax before the flames.'"[15]

And to repeat an earlier passage from Maria herself:

"I felt that I had a great work to perform; and was in haste to make a profession of my faith in Christ, that I might be about my Father's business. Soon after I made this profession, The Spirit of God came before me, and I spake before many … A something said within my breast, 'Press forward, I will be with thee.' And my heart made this reply, 'Lord, if thou wilt be with me, then I will speak for thee as long as I live.' And thus far I have every reason to believe that it is the divine influence of the Holy Spirit operating upon my heart that could possibly induce me to make the feeble and unworthy efforts that I have."[16]

In her farewell address to African Americans in Boston, she wrote:

"It has actually appeared to me at different periods as though the powers of earth and hell had combined against me, to prove my overthrow. Yet amidst their dire attempts, I have found the Almighty to be 'a friend that sticketh closer than a brother [Proverbs 18:24].' He never will forsake the soul that leans on him; though he chastens and corrects it, it is for the soul's best interest …

But some of you have said, 'do not talk so much about religion, the people do not wish to hear you. We know these things. Tell us something we do not know.' If you know these things, my dear friends, and have performed them, far happier, and more prosperous would you now have been … I have, regardless of the frowns and scoffs of a guilty world, plead up religion, and the pure principles of morality among you. Religion is the most glorious theme that mortals can converse upon … It is that fountain that has no end, and those that drink thereof shall never thirst; for it is, indeed, a well of water springing up in the soul unto everlasting life."[17]

Maria Stewart is surely an example of a "constant crossing of boundaries between religion and social action" providing "an example of 'lived religion' that acted and didn't wait for things to change."[18]

## Sites to Visit in Massachusetts

Home of Maria Stewart
81 Joy Street
Boston, MA 02108
*This is not the original building, but this is where Maria and James Stewart lived after David Walker and his wife, Eliza, purchased a new home.*

African Meeting House
46 Joy Street
Boston, MA 02108
*Maria was married here, was a member of the church, and delivered speeches here including her 1833 farewell address to Boston's African American community.*

Franklin Hall
16 Franklin Street
Boston, MA 02111
*The New-England Anti-Slavery Society met here, and Maria spoke here in 1832 and 1833.*

Offices of the *Liberator* (site of)
12 Post Office Square
Boston, MA 02109
*Maria formed a powerful partnership with William Lloyd Garrison, the editor of the* Liberator. *He published almost everything she wrote.*

## Resources

*Maria W. Stewart: America's First Black Woman Political Writer* by Marilyn Richardson (Indiana University Press, 1987).

*Word, Like Fire: Maria Stewart, the Bible, and the Rights of African Americans* by Valerie C. Cooper (University of Virginia Press, 2012).

*Early Negro Writing, 1760-1837* by Dorothy Porter Wesley (Black Classic Press, 1995).

*Black Feminist Thought: Knowledge, Consciousness and the Politics of Empowerment* by Patricia Hill Collins (Routledge Classics, 1990).

*Black Women in America: An Historical Encyclopedia* by Darlene Clark Hine, ed. (Indiana University Press, 1994).

*African-American Orators* by Richard W. Leeman (Greenwood, 1996).

Websites:
*Search for Maria Stewart at:*
About.com
Boston Women's Heritage Trail
Wikipedia.org

## Notes to the Biographical Sketch

1    Maria Stewart: *America's First Black Woman Political Writer* by Marilyn Richardson (Indiana University Press, 1987), xiv.
2    Ibid., 3.

3　Ibid.
4　Ibid., 6.
5　Ibid., 7.
6　About.com.
7　Richardson, xiii.
8　Ibid., 68.
9　Ibid., xiii.
10　Ibid., and 70.
11　Ibid., 66-7.
12　Ibid., 70-1.
13　Ibid., xix.
14　Ibid., 79.
15　Ibid., xvii.
16　Ibid., 66-7.
17　Ibid., 71-2.
18　*Standing Before Us: Unitarian Universalist Women and Social Reform, 1776–1936* by Dorothy May Emerson (Skinner House Books, 2000), 11.

"If I would be true to myself, true to my Heavenly Father, I must be actuated by high and holy principles, and pursue that course of conduct which, to me, appears best calculated to promote the highest good of the world. Because I know that I shall suffer, shall I for this, like Lot's wife, turn back? No, Mother, if in this hour of the world's need I should refuse to lend my aid, however small it might be, I should have no right to think myself a Christian, and I should forever despise Lucy Stone."

—*Lucy Stone, to her mother, 1846*

# Lucy Stone

### (1803–1893)

---

## Her Achievements

- First woman in America to graduate from college
- First woman in America to keep her own name after getting married
- First woman in New England to be cremated
- Influential leader of the women's rights and woman suffrage movements
- Influential leader of the abolitionist movement
- Editor of a national newspaper (*Woman's Journal*)
- Early and effective female public speaker
- Mother of Alice Stone Blackwell, another pioneer in the woman suffrage movement and newspaper editor

---

## Her Story

What amazes and saddens me is to know is that Lucy Stone struggled with depression, migraine headaches, and feelings of inadequacy her entire life, which is not unheard of among the leaders of pivotal political movements. But despite these challenges, she pushed on with a singleness of purpose that's an inspiration to anyone.

Lucy Stone was born on August 13, 1818, on her family's farm on Coy's Hill in rural West Brookfield, Massachusetts. She was the eighth of nine siblings, and her father ruled his wife and children by "divine right"—meaning that men were in charge and women were not important. There was "only one will" and it was his. He drank, beat his children, and insulted Lucy's looks. Lucy was afraid of him, and as Andrea Moore Kerr, her biographer, points out, some of Lucy's behavior later in life was typical of abused children.[1]

Lucy watched her mother work terribly hard, and even beg her husband for money. When Lucy became politically active on behalf of women, she always kept her mother in mind. At a young age, Lucy decided to never marry. As she wrote years later, "Though it is sad and desolate to live unmarried, it is worse to be a thing."[2]

Lucy's brothers were schooled; she was not, initially, even though she was, by all accounts, smarter than they were. Still, she read what she could, and craved an education. The Bible and the *Worcester Spy*, the local newspaper, provided the only reading material in her home. But little by little Lucy found ways to let books creep in. At some point, she was allowed to attend a one-room district school taught by Thomas Coney who used to beat his students.

The children were expected to work hard on the farm and Lucy took in piecework as well from a local leather factory to help support the family. Then, as a willful teenager, and despite her father's disapproval, she sat in on some of her brothers' college tutorials. She determined to learn Greek and Hebrew some day to be able to read the Bible in its original form. At the Congregational church she attended with her family, she heard constant Biblical references to women's inferiority and prescribed roles, and she just didn't believe it.

Lucy's world changed in the early 1830s when the railroad opened connecting West Brookfield and Worcester to Boston and Albany, New York. Famous political speakers arrived, including Frances Wright who spoke on educational opportunities for girls and women and the abuses of marriage such as property rights. Lucy was thirteen at the time, and while the Stones did not attend Frances Wright's speech her messages were in the public arena for discussion. Lucy made up her mind to go to college, and famously started collecting chestnuts to sell for money to buy textbooks. Meanwhile, her older brothers were of college age. They went off to school, and returned home with inspiring stories.

When Lucy was sixteen, she heard Mary Lyon speak before a local sewing circle. Mary was the founder of the Mount Holyoke Female Seminary in South Hadley, Massachusetts, and spent considerable time "on the road" speaking about the value of female education, recruiting students, and raising funds. Later that year, Lucy took a teaching job in New Braintree, Massachusetts, and was furious to learn how much less women teachers were paid than their male counterparts. Later, she taught school in Paxton. While most of her money had to be sent home to her father, she was able to keep enough to attend classes and continue her studies.

## Education

Lucy was probably nineteen or twenty when she first read the anti-slavery writings of Sarah and Angelina Grimké thanks to her brother Bowman's subscription to the abolitionist newspaper the *Liberator*. She was profoundly affected by these two young Southern Quaker women who had witnessed slavery first-hand and were now touring the country to present petitions before state legislatures to end slavery—and even speaking in public, which women did not do in the 1830s. In fact, in 1833, Angelina Grimké became the first woman in America to address a state legislature—in Massachusetts. Along with the Grimkés' work, Lucy also read William Lloyd Garrison, Lydia Maria Child, Abby Kelley Foster, Maria Stewart, and so many others who were part of the Boston abolitionist group. She was inspired.

But Lucy was also outraged that year when the minister of her Congregational church read a pastoral letter one Sunday denouncing women speakers. A deacon of the church invited Abby Kelley Foster to speak in rebuttal. The minister was put "on trial" by the congregation, but Lucy, as a female member, was not allowed to vote.

Despite her father's objections to Lucy pursuing an education versus trying to find a husband, she earned enough money by teaching that she was able to attend the Mount Holyoke Female Seminary in 1838. Unfortunately, the death of her sister, Eliza, forced her to abandon her studies to take care of her nieces and her distraught mother. But she did attend the nearby "select school" of Alfred Bartlett who supported women's rights and encouraged Lucy to begin her study of Latin and Greek. He also gave her a copy of an early essay by Sarah Grimké on female equality. But, once again, she had to abandon her studies to care for another ill sister, Rhoda, and to take over her sister's teaching job in Paxton. Rhoda died in 1839. Lucy returned home, but the following year she continued her studies at the Wilbraham Academy and then returned to the Quaboag Seminary to prepare for her entrance exams to Oberlin College.

By August of 1843, at age twenty-five, Lucy had saved enough money through teaching to attend Oberlin College—the first college to admit women and African Americans—and she left the family farm to begin her new life. She made the five-day journey to Ohio by train, ferry, steam ship, and stage coach. Before long, however, she clashed with college policy and her professors because they refused to allow women to participate in rhetoric (speaking) classes and debates. She wanted equal access to all courses and was told that because it was "improper and impossible" for women to participate equally in the work force her demands were absurd. Lucy won the admiration of her fellow (and sister) students and was the subject of much discussion.[3]

During her four years at Oberlin, Lucy taught at the college's school for fugitive slaves and freedmen. From them, she learned first-hand about the evils of slavery.

She taught them trigonometry, Greek, Latin, Hebrew, astronomy, chemistry, geology, biology, natural philosophy, logic, rhetoric, and the Bible. In her second year, she began to publish articles and letters in reform publications.

## Speaking

In her third year, 1846, the future Antoinette Brown Blackwell, the first woman in America to be ordained as a minister, audited rhetoric classes with Lucy. They were "rebuked," and formed their own debating society to practice what they both knew they were called to do. On August 1, 1846, Lucy gave her first public address to a local anti-slavery society despite terrible headaches and self-doubt. Her speech was reported in the local newspaper.

In 1847, as graduation approached, Oberlin students voted Lucy valedictorian, which meant she would give the valedictory address. But the college administration would not allow her to speak, and insisted on having a male professor read her address. Lucy refused. She was twenty-nine when she graduated, and that year she met William Lloyd Garrison and Stephen Foster Douglass who were in Oberlin for an anti-slavery rally. The men were so taken with her speaking ability they invited her speak on behalf of the New England Anti-Slavery Society in Boston. But it took weeks for arrangements to be made, and, meanwhile, Lucy accepted a teaching position in North Brookfield to earn money.

Back in her home territory, Lucy's brother, Bowman, who was now the minister of the Evangelical Congregational Church in Gardner, Massachusetts, invited her to speak on the rights of women at his church. Her speech, delivered in October 1847 and titled "The Province of Women," launched Lucy's public speaking career. Every other member of Lucy's family disapproved of her address, but the reporters who attended along with the audience commented on her extraordinary voice, the command she held over people, her use of everyday language versus the usual flowery oratory of public speakers, and the fact that she told stories from real life.

In 1848, Sarah Grimké published the groundbreaking *Letters on the Equality of the Sexes* which Lucy read. And, finally, she heard from the New England Anti-Slavery Society (NEASS). Lucy left North Brookfield to work for them as a paid speaker. Her parents were adamantly opposed, perhaps out of concern for her safety but perhaps not. Regardless of their wishes, Lucy set off. The first speech she gave was in Waterford, Massachusetts. After that, she spoke at churches, town halls, schoolhouses and outdoors in picnic groves. She spoke without a script. By Fall, Lucy was appearing on posters with William Lloyd Garrison and Wendell Phillips. She met "everyone" in Boston, including Elizabeth Peabody who invited her to speak at the evening salons in Boston that attracted Transcendentalists, foreign dignitaries, and politicians.

While abolition was close to Lucy's heart, so were women's rights, and she made an agreement with NEASS to speak against slavery on weekends and on behalf of women during weekdays. Initially, Lucy took up collections after her women's rights talks to pay for posters and pamphlets and to avoid having to charge admission. But that changed as her finances dwindled, and hundreds of people at a time gladly paid an admission fee to hear Lucy speak. By 1848, following her appearance at the Women's Rights Convention in Seneca Falls, New York, Lucy was attracting crowds of 2,000-3,000 people. In 1850, at the first annual Women's Rights Convention in Worcester, despite a sudden illness, Lucy appeared at the opening ceremony.

In 1850, following the passage of the Fugitive Slave Law, Lucy declared that if having slavery was the only way to hold the Union together the United States deserved to fail and Northerners should instead form a Northern Republic. When the escaped slave Anthony Burns was captured in Boston that year and returned to the South, Lucy gave a "rousing speech" against his arrest in the so-called "Cradle of Liberty" (Boston) and predicted that war was inevitable.[5]

Lucy helped organize and she spoke at the second annual Women's Rights Convention in Worcester in 1851. Her speech received national press coverage. At the convention, she met Susan B. Anthony, Elizabeth Cady Stanton, and Amelia Bloomer, after which Lucy started wearing the "Bloomer dress," which resembled puffy pants, and she began to attract negative attention for her inappropriate attire.

### Self-doubt

That same year, in Boston, Lucy met Henry Blackwell, who had recently heard her speak. Henry (called "Harry"), was the brother of Dr. Elizabeth Blackwell, the first woman physician in the United States. Harry has been described as ambitious, desirous of money but wreckless with it, and a risk taker, but also compassionate—and he was an abolitionist. Henry launched a campaign to win Lucy's hand in marriage. He swore he would not interfere with her work, but very quickly, before they were married, Lucy was lending him money to make up for his constant losses. Lucy was wary of Henry, never forgetting her mother's experience and ever mindful of current marriage laws that made a woman, her children, and her property the property of the husband. Henry insisted they would have a different kind of marriage.[6]

On May 1, 1855, Lucy and Harry were married at Coy's Hill by a Unitarian minister. Newspapers reported "the death of Lucy Stone," but she had determined to keep her last name and the two wrote a protest against current marriage laws which they read it at their ceremony and published it in newspapers.

But the marriage suffered almost immediately. Lucy became insecure on stage. Harry insisted on moving to Cincinnati where he had new business interests. Lucy still did some speaking in New England and Wisconsin, but she felt the strain of the more traditional role she was being asked to play along with the fact that they were going through her savings. Lucy was back in New England in 1856 to care for yet another sick relative, and there she met the author Ralph Waldo Emerson and the progressive newspaper editor Horace Greeley. She enlisted their support in her women's rights platform.[7]

While Lucy had been plagued by self-doubt since her marriage, she now felt her confidence returning. As she wrote, "Every day … getting back more and more the old faith in myself and brave courage too, which before helped me to work out all that which made me better, and was good for others too." Lucy was pregnant the following winter, but she kept working. Harry was not at all happy with her decision. Lucy was worried about her diminishing health and how her work might make her feel worse, but they needed the money she earned. Lucy was now speaking in public forums and before state legislatures.[8]

Lucy gave birth to Alice Stone Blackwell in 1857 at a farm she and Harry had bought in Orange, New Jersey. He was away at the time. Later that year, Lucy refused to pay property taxes because she was not represented as a voter. The town seized objects of hers to auction off. Lucy returned to a modest lecture schedule, but, again, Harry was not happy. Meanwhile, he was selling land without her knowledge, and becoming embroiled in lawsuits. They moved to Bloomfield, New Jersey, where there was more land for crops to feed the family. Lucy went to Chicago with Harry, but by now she was very depressed and returned to Coy's Hill to care for her ill mother. Ironically, in 1860, at that year's Women's Rights Convention, Susan B. Anthony put forth the idea that divorce was a woman's right. Lucy was unable to attend.

## Suffrage

In 1861, leaving baby Alice with her family at Coy's Hill, Lucy returned to a full speaking schedule. It had a "tonic effect" on her. She wrote, "I am so glad to find again the old inspiration, and it comes to me more and more." But both her guilt and the outbreak of the Civil War brought her home. She and Harry were now spending most of their time apart. As Andrea Moore Kerr explains, she blamed herself for their problems. But it was clear that his behavior impacted her health and her self-confidence. After the war ended, Lucy agreed to move to Roseville, New Jersey, with Harry and Alice to try and save her marriage. Harry wanted power and money, she wanted to return to Boston to be useful. And she did go to Boston, placed Alice in a good school, and resumed her suffrage work.[9]

There was talk that year of merging black and woman suffrage into one cause under the National Equal Rights Society, but with African Americans facing enormous backlash after the war, and without a clear way to exclude the word "male" from an amendment to ensure African American male suffrage (which Frederick Douglass famously called a matter of life and death), the women's movement split in two. Elizabeth Cady Stanton and Susan B. Anthony (henceforward called Stanton and Anthony), who refused to work for suffrage if women were not included, held their own convention that year. Lucy, quite ill from stress headaches and Harry's latest financial exploits, left for Gardner with Alice to be with her family.

Lucy, along with women like Julia Ward Howe, did not wish to divide the black and woman suffrage issue and Lucy spoke to both issues in New York City in 1867 where she had traveled with Harry. Asking states and territories to consider both forms of suffrage was a political minefield. Some women suffragists were using anti-Black language. Kansas, for example defeated both forms of suffrage because African Americans were included in the proposed legislation. George Francis Train started a racist newspaper called the *Revolution* and sided with Stanton and Anthony. Lucy distanced herself from them, and spoke on behalf of the American Equal Rights Association in

New York, New Jersey, Ohio, and New England. In 1868, Lucy attempted to vote in New Jersey, but her ballot was rejected. She took to the public stage to protest.

In November of that year Lucy was in Boston to found the New England Woman Suffrage Association (NEWSA). Julia Ward Howe was named president. Stanton and Anthony did not attend because they knew this organization was designed to replace their own. In 1869, Lucy was in Washington, D.C., to lobby for universal suffrage although she "remained staunchly and publicly committed to full enfranchisement for African Americans, even if it meant securing rights for blacks before women." That February, the 15th Amendment passed giving African American men the right to vote. Stanton and Anthony had mounted a campaign to prevent its passage and failed.[10]

Harry was now seeing another woman, and there was talk of marital separation. Lucy simply overshadowed him. She now traveled relentlessly, organizing, visiting newspaper editors, and placing columns. She believed in the power of the press to sway public opinion. She also started planning a national suffrage organization, which Stanton and Anthony were doing as well. She moved to Boston, regardless of whether Harry would follow, and placed Alice in a school in nearby Newburyport. In Ohio, in 1869, Lucy Stone and others launched the American Woman Suffrage Association (AWSA). Its purpose was "to gain the vote for women by state action and through amendments to state constitutions." Lucy trained others how to organize, run meetings, arrange publicity, advertise meetings, obtain and distribute material, and persuade local suffrage groups to join the national organization.[11]

On January 8, 1870, Lucy launched the *Woman's Journal* in Boston, which was "designed to support and publicize the policies and activities initially of the AWSA and then of the movement as a whole." Mary Ashton Rice Livermore served as the first (paid) editor. The *Journal* was paid for by shares purchased by such people as Angelina and Sarah Grimké, William Lloyd Garrison, and Julia Ward Howe. Five thousand copies of the *Journal* were printed and distributed, claiming its devotion to the "interest of Woman, to her educational, industrial, legal and Political Equality." Lucy Stone found subscribers, gathered news, kept accounts of salaries, raised funds, obtained letters of endorsement, found advertisers, laid out the newspaper, worked with printers, and oversaw mailing and distribution. The *Journal* sold out. Subscriptions poured in.[12]

1870 was an eventful year. Annie, Lucy's adopted daughter died. A reconciliation between the two suffrage groups was attempted but failed. Virginia Woodhull ran for president—the first woman in America to do so. The 16th Amendment was proposed to allow women to vote nationally. Out West, women were already doing so. Lucy organized the Massachusetts Woman Suffrage Association (MWSA) and addressed that year's Massachusetts Republican Convention. Tactically, there was more focus now on forming committees, using straw polls, and lobbying compared to the suffragists' earlier use of moral suasion. Slowly, towns and cities began to let women vote in municipal elections. At the end of that year, Stanton and Anthony completed a history of the woman suffrage movement and relegated Lucy's role to mere lines.

Lucy spoke at the Women's Rights Convention in 1871,

which was held that year in Washington, D.C. Virginia Woodhull spoke about female sexuality in ways that "confirmed" for many that suffrage would lead to free love and promiscuity. Many suffragists felt that she set back the movement. Lucy and Harry reconciled that year, and he began to help her with the *Journal*. Lucy was now writing or recruiting most of the content, including fiction, and it allowed her to introduce writers like Lydia Maria Child.

On December 15, 1873, Lucy and others celebrated the 100th anniversary of the Boston Tea Party at a gala gathering at Boston's Faneuil Hall. Lucy's speech decried men's ability to tax women, to judge them, even hang them, to take their property and their children. Women had no legal voice—no representation.

Lucy was now in her late fifties, unwell, weathered by many disappointments and infidelity, but she still had her purpose—the power of the ballot. Her family counted on her for financial and emotional support. While Lucy was the politician, Harry was the "ornamental partner" for whom she had to find a role. Alice, a teenager who had grown up as the daughter of a celebrity, took an interest in her mother's cause. Lucy now organized small suffrage clubs to shift the movement from large public arenas to small private ones—to the parlors of women like Julia Ward Howe. The gatherings were reported in local newspapers. Women wanted to attend to be in the presence of women like Julia—even reporters and legislators were invited. The movement now saw the "confluence of the political and social."[13]

In the late 1870s, the AWSA was organized into districts, each with its own political action group that lobbied locally. The Boston office sent supporting materials. The focus was now entirely on local and state activities rather than national. A federal amendment for woman suffrage would have to be ratified by each state. Lucy urged suffragists not to neglect actions in the states. Now, with the increased number of immigrant women arriving, the movement was accused of being gentrified—meaning, exclusively for middle and upper middle class white women. Lucy explained that the ballot would improve conditions for working women at all class levels and from all backgrounds. But it was an uphill battle to include the working class women. Many were too busy or felt too oppressed by working conditions to get involved.

Still, the *Woman's Journal* increasingly addressed labor issues, child welfare, and Jim Crow laws in the South. It also included international news about women. People in all thirty-nine states now subscribed, and Lucy was still running the show and raising money to pay for the *Journal*.

Lucy attended the famous Centennial Exhibition in Philadelphia in 1876, and brought with her an exhibit on taxation without representation. Elizabeth Cady Stanton requested biographical information from Lucy for the second volume on the history of the woman suffrage movement. But Lucy still felt betrayed by Volume I and sent only minimal text. Alice Stone Blackwell entered Boston University that Fall, still interested in all of her mother's causes—including higher education for women. Lucy and Harry traveled to Colorado to witness a state-wide vote for woman suffrage. Lucy now saw the role of the *Journal* as a press agent for other organizations.

In 1861, Massachusetts allowed women to vote for school committee. Lucy registered as "Lucy Stone" but her application was annulled because she had failed to use her married name. Despite recurring ill health and more financial troubles with Harry, Lucy continued to speak in the 1870s and 1880s. After graduating from Boston University, Alice joined the staff of the *Journal*. Increasingly, with so many of the "old guard" gone, many people questioned the need for two national suffrage organizations. In 1881 and 1882, the two volumes of Stanton and Anthony's "history" were published. Lucy and the AWSA were barely mentioned. Then, opposition to woman suffrage grew in 1883 as Catholic priests condemned women for wanting to threatening their families by seeking the vote.

On the 50th anniversary of Oberlin College in 1883, Lucy was invited to speak—and she did.

## Closing

The late 1880s brought Lucy to a school for black children in Georgia, where she had gone to restore her health. A merger between the two suffrage organizations was attempted, and failed again. Stanton and Anthony planned an anniversary celebration of the Seneca Falls convention in 1888. In 1890, Lucy Stone and others planned a celebration in Worcester to mark the first national women's rights convention.

In the 1890s, Lucy was fairly worn out. She received house guests in the home she had purchased at Copp's Hill in Dorchester (now part of Boston), but she did rise to the occasion of attending the Chicago World's Fair in

1891. That year, she was invited to the White House to have tea with Anna Harrison, the president's wife, and other suffragists. (They had come a long way and were now respectable.) The sculptor Anne Whitney carved a portrait bust of Lucy for the 1892 Chicago World's Fair. And in 1893, despite her obvious frailty, Lucy went with Alice to speak before the World's Congress of Representative Women, an international organization that was tracing the recent path of the women's rights movement that year and celebrating everything that had been achieved.

As a result of years of hard work, Lucy noted:

"We have women's clubs, the Woman's Congress, women's educational and industrial unions, the moral education societies, the Woman's Relief Corps, police matrons, the Woman's Christian Temperance Union, colleges for women,  and co-educational colleges, and the Harvard Annex, medical schools and medical societies open to women, women's hospitals, women in the pulpit, women as a power in the press, authors, women artists, women's beneficent societies and Helping Hand societies, women school supervisors, and factory inspectors and prison inspectors, women on state boards of charity, the International Council of Women, the Woman's National Council, and last, but not least, the Board of Lady Managers."[14]

After she read each item, the women in the audience applauded "long and loud."[15]

Returning home, it was clear to Lucy that she was dying and she went to stay with her cousin Emma in Gardner.

She started to say goodbye to old friends. Lucy Stone died on October 18 with Alice by her side. Lucy's last words to her daughter were, "Make the world better." The church building where Lucy's funeral took place on October 21 was packed with hundreds standing outside. An old, unnamed opponent observed, "The death of no woman in America had ever called out so general a tribute of public respect and esteem." Lengthy tributes appeared in newspapers in America and Europe. Six women and six men pallbearers carried her casket. Finally, Lucy was conveyed to Forest Hills Cemetery in Jamaica Plain where she was cremated and buried.[16]

Lucy Stone was the first woman in New England to be cremated. In death, the cemetery carved the name on her tomb as "Lucy Stone Blackwell." Alice Stone Blackwell wrote her mother's biography, and witnessed the passage of the 19th Amendment in 1920 guaranteeing women the right to vote.

### Her Faith in Action

Raised in the orthodox Congregational church in West Brookfield, Massachusetts, Lucy heard many sermons that claimed Biblical "proof" of women's inherent inferiority. She didn't believe it for a minute, and decided to learn Latin and Greek to be able to read the Bible in its original.

Later, at Oberlin College, she was "required to attend religious services and prayer meetings ... presided over by Charles Finney, the 'hell-fire and brimstone' preacher of the Second Great Awakening," according to Elea Kemler, one of Lucy's biographers. She "grew more and more disillusioned with the church of her upbringing.

She declared herself Unitarian and remained dedicated to Unitarian principles until her death." These included a commitment to individual improvement along with an activist/social justice agenda to "make the world better," as she instructed her daughter on her death bed.[17]

Lucy's activism on behalf of others could not be more clear, even at a time when women were not supposed to do certain things like speak in public. Her commitment to women's rights and to African American rights drove her to make a difference despite recurring illnesses, a difficult marriage, and recurring self doubt.

We can see the role Lucy's faith played in this letter she wrote to her mother in 1846 during her last year at Oberlin College, when she had decided to become a public speaker (this is an excerpt).

"I surely would not be a public speaker if I chose a life of ease, for it will be a laborious one; nor would I do it for the sake of honor, for I know that I will be disesteemed, nay, even hated, by some who are now my friends, or who profess to be …

If I would be true to myself, true to my Heavenly Father, I must be actuated by high and holy principles, and pursue that course of conduct which, to me, appears best calculated to promote the highest good of the world. Because I know that I shall suffer, shall I for this, like Lot's wife, turn back? No, Mother, if in this hour of the world's need I should refuse to lend my aid, however small it might be, I should have no right to think myself a Christian, and I should forever despise Lucy Stone …

If, while I hear the wild shriek of the slave mother robbed of her little ones, or the muffled groan of the daughter spoiled of her virtue, I do not open my mouth for the dumb, am I not guilty? Or should I go, as you said, from house to house to do it, when I could tell so many more in less time, if they should be gathered in one place? You would not object, or think it wrong, for a man to plead the cause of the suffering and the outcast; and surely the moral character of the act is not changed because it is done by a woman …

There are no trials so great as they suffer who neglect or refuse to do what they believe is their duty. I expect to plead not for the slave only, but for suffering humanity everywhere. Especially do I mean to labor for the elevation of my sex."[18]

## Sites to Visit in Massachusetts

<u>Birthplace of Lucy Stone (site of)</u>
Coy's Hill
Route 9
West Brookfield, MA 01585

<u>Burying Place of Lucy Stone</u>
Forest Hills Cemetery
95 Forest Hills Avenue
Jamaica Plain, Massachusetts 02130

<u>Offices of the *Woman's Journal*</u>
9 Park Street
Boston, MA 02111
*The building still stands, in fill view of the State House.*

<u>Boston Women's Memorial</u>
Commonwealth Avenue Mall at Gloucester Street
Boston, MA 02116
*The Memorial features Abigail Adams, Lucy Stone, and Phillis Wheatley.*

## Resources

*Lucy Stone: Speaking Out for Equality* by Andrea Moore Kerr (Rutgers University Press, 1995).

*Lucy Stone: Pioneer of Women's Rights* by Alice Stone Blackwell (Little, Brown, 1930).

*Morning Star: A Biography of Lucy Stone, 1818-1893* by Elinor Rice Hays (Harcourt, 1961).

*Standing Before Us: Unitarian Universalist Women and Social Reform, 1776—1936* by Dorothy May Emerson (Skinner House Books, 2000).

<u>Websites</u>
*Search for Lucy Stone at:*
About.com
Boston Women's Heritage Trail
Massachusetts Center for the Book

## Notes to the Biographical Sketch

1   *Lucy Stone: Speaking Out for Equality* by Andrea Moore Kerr (Rutgers University Press, 1995), 9, 13-15.
2   Ibid., 57.
3   Ibid., 31.
4   Ibid., 37.
5   Ibid., 56.

6   Ibid. 66.
7   Ibid., 101.
8   Ibid.
9   Ibid., 113, 119.
10  "Lucy Stone Biographical Sketch" by Elea Kemler
    in *Standing Before Us: Unitarian Universalist Women
    and Social Reform, 1776—1936* by Dorothy May
    Emerson, ed. (Skinner House Books, 2000), 33.
11  Ibid., 146-7, and Kemler, 33.
12  Kemler, 33-4, and Kerr, 149.
13  Ibid., 184, 192.
14  Ibid., 239-40.
15  Ibid.
16  Ibid., 4-7.
17  Kemler, 32.
18  Reprinted in Emerson, pp. 30-1.

"I, young in life, by seeming cruel fate
Was snatch'd from Afric's fancy'd happy seat:
What pangs excruciating must molest,
What sorrows labour in my parent's breast?
Steel'd was that soul and by no misery mov'd
That from a father seiz'd his babe belov'd:
Such, such my case. And can I then but pray
Others may never feel tyrannic sway?

'Twas mercy brought me from my pagan land,
Taught my benighted soul to understand
That there's a God—that there's a Saviour too;
Once I redemption neither sought nor knew.
Some view our sable race with scornful eye –
'Their color is a diabolical dye.'
Remember, Christians, Negroes black as Cain
May be refined, and join the angelic train."

—*Phillis Wheatley*

# Phillis Wheatley

### (ca. 1753–1784)

---

### Her Achievements

- First African American poet
- First female African American poet
- First enslaved poet
- Considered the earliest contributor to the African American literary tradition
- Stood up to the racism of Christian ministers
- Survived the Atlantic crossing and being held as an enslaved girl/woman

---

## Her Story

Phillis Wheatley's story captured my heart years ago
when I first heard about this young slave girl who became
America's first African American published poet, took on
Christian ministers, met royalty in England, and then died
in poverty and obscurity in an unmarked grave in Boston
at about the age of thirty. It's such a poignant story, at
once courageous and tragic. If you're ever in Boston,
I hope you will visit the display about her at Old South
Meeting House where she was a member. It features a
lovely, petite, life-sized statue of her, standing right next to
you, that will take your breath away.

The young girl, whose real name we don't know, was
born around 1753 in West Africa. Historians disagree
on exactly where. Vincent Carretta, Phillis Wheatley's
most recent biographer, tells us the language of the Fula
people, who dominated the region, wrote in Arabic and
Phillis was probably already learning to write when she
was kidnapped at about the age of seven and shipped to
America. Surrounded by death, disease, and violence,
Phillis somehow survived the "horrifying trauma of the
Middle Passage" and arrived at Griffin's Wharf in Boston
in 1761 where she was put up for auction by John Avery.[1]

In her only partially autobiographical poem, Phillis wrote
to the Earl of Dartmouth:

"I, young in life, by seeming cruel fate
Was snatch'd from Afric's fancy'd happy seat:
What pangs excruciating must molest,
What sorrows labour in my parent's breast?
Steel'd was that soul and by no misery mov'd

That from a father seiz'd his babe belov'd:
Such, such my case. And can I then but pray
Others may never feel tyrannic sway?"[2]

Susanna Wheatley, who had recently pronounced her
desire to "live the life and die the death of a good Christian
woman," according to Phillis's biographer William Henry
Robinson, "was eager to purchase a young, trainable
African girl to attend to her personally in her remaining
years." She "spied a nearly naked and obviously sick, but
winsome, brown-eyed black child … by virtue of having
shed her front teeth, she was reckoned to have been
between seven and eight years of age." Mrs. Wheatley
was "smitten at once by the docile child and procured her
for a trifle (ten pounds sterling)" because the auctioneer
feared she could easily die.[3]

John Wheatley, Susanna's husband, owned a shop on
busy King Street as well as a schooner, warehouses,
wharves, and rental property. The Wheatley mansion
was also located on King Street, in the heart of Boston's
downtown. The surviving Wheatley children were
Nathaniel and Mary. Susanna had lost three children,
including a daughter who would have been Phillis's age.

Mary Wheatley wanted to teach school, and her first pupil,
at Susanna's insistence, was Phillis. Phillis read the Bible
and books in the family library. She was also allowed to
peruse the libraries of Wheatley family friends where she
could study classical literature, history, geography, politics,
English literature, Greek, and Latin. She read stories
about ancient leaders, and translated long story poems
from ancient texts and British poets. Susanna kept her
supplied with pen and paper so she could begin to write.

In fact, according to William Robinson, "Mrs. Wheatley lovingly devoted the rest of her life in behalf of the talented black girl," becoming "more of a servant to the girl than the girl became a servant to her." Phillis was excused from most domestic chores and given an attic room in the Wheatley mansion with a light (other "servants" lived in the carriage house), a bedside quill, and a supply of ink and paper to write down immediately whatever stray poetic thoughts might flit through her consciousness at night."[4]

## Writing

Phillis was about twelve when she began her writing career in 1765 by writing a poetical letter to a Wheatley family friend, the Mohegan Indian Christian minister Rev. Samson Occom who was traveling in Europe at the time. Later that year, she composed her first poem, "On the Death of the Rev. Dr. Sewell when Sick," written in honor of the pastor of Old South Meeting House. Phillis drew her ideas from what was around her—particularly current events, religion, and discussions about liberty. A poem she wrote in 1766 to King George of England celebrated the end of the Stamp Act.

Phillis's first published poem appeared in the December 21, 1767 edition of the *Newport Mercury* of Newport, Rhode Island. Titled "On Messrs. Hussey and Coffin," the poem told the story of a storm off Cape Cod, Massachusetts, and two men who survived a shipwreck. The Wheatleys vacationed in Newport, so it is likely that Susanna arranged for the poem's publication. According to William Robinson, she "tirelessly promoted the girl's poetic career."[5]

In September 1768, when British troops arrived in Boston, Phillis wrote the poem "On the Arrival of the Ships of War, and Landing of the Troops." When troops stoned the house of an American "rebel" and an eleven-year-old boy was killed in the chaos, she described the incident in another poem. She decried the "Bloody Massacre," or the Boston Massacre, on March 5 when the African American Crispus Attucks was killed.

Phillis's fame grew far beyond Boston when her elegiac poem marking the death of the evangelical Methodist preacher George Whitefield was published in numerous newspapers and as a broadside, or poster. Whitefield had been the private chaplain to Selina Hastings, the Countess of Huntingdon, in England, who took notice of Phillis's work. Phillis now enjoyed continental (American) and transatlantic fame.

Susanna Wheatley chose August 18, 1771, as the day for Phillis to be baptized in the Old South Meeting House because it was the anniversary of the day Susanna purchased her in 1761. The baptismal year would have marked her "coming of age" as a teenager. Old South was located at the corner of what is now Washington and Milk Streets, just a few city blocks from the Wheatley home.

## Fame

This was an odd time for Phillis. She enjoyed fame as a published poet, recited her poetry to guests in the Wheatley home, or accepted invitations to speak in the homes of prominent Bostonians. And yet, she was a enslaved. As Maryann N. Weidt describes her situation, "Phillis must have felt caught between two worlds"—not allowed to associate with the other slaves, and yet not free, like the white people with whom she mingled."[6]

Now, Susanna wanted Phillis to publish a book of her poems. Susanna advertised for subscribers in the *Boston Censor*, but she did not attract enough people to pay for the book's publication. She then contacted the Countess of Huntingdon in England for her support, as well as the publisher Archibald Bell in London as no Boston printer would publish the work of a slave. Archibald Bell required "proof" that Phillis had written the book, so Susanna contacted eighteen prominent (white, male) citizens of Boston, including the governor and lieutenant governor, who interrogated Phillis.

This was not at all unusual. At the time debates were raging about whether or not Africans were part of the human race and could think for themselves or just imitate whites. As historian Henry Louis Gates, Jr. explains, "All of this helps us to understand why Wheatley's oral examination was so important. If she had indeed written her poems, then this would demonstrate that Africans were human beings and should be liberated from slavery. If, on the other hand, she had not written, or could not write her poems, or if indeed she was like a parrot who speaks a few words plainly, then that would be another matter entirely. Essentially, she was auditioning for the humanity of the entire African people."[7]

During her interrogation, Phillis clearly demonstrated her knowledge of scripture, ancient texts, great literature, history, philosophy, theology, and current events because the eighteen men signed a statement testifying to her ability. Their statement appeared at the beginning of

Phillis's book:

"To the Public. We, whose names are under-written, do assure the World, that the Poems specified in the following pages were (as we verily believe) written by Phillis, a young Negro girl, who was but a few years since brought an uncultivated barbarian from Africa, and has ever since been, and now is, under the disadvantage of serving as a slave in a family in this Town. She has been examined by some of the best judges, and is thought qualified to write them."[8]

On May 8, 1773, at age nineteen, Phillis sailed to London with Nathaniel Wheatley, Susanna's son, to witness the printing of her book, which Susanna and Phillis had agreed would be dedicated to the Countess of Huntingdon. The Countess agreed to their request, and insisted on paying for an engraved likeness of Phillis for the book. The engraving was probably copied after a painting by Scipio Moorehead in Boston, a talented black slave of the Presbyterian Reverend John Moorehead, "whose wife, Mary, instructed Bostonians in art and guided Scipio in his drawing." At the time, it was highly unusual to have an image of an identifiable African American woman.[9]

Phillis's journey to London was reported in newspapers throughout America, noting the impending publication of "the extraordinary negro poetess." And even though Susanna was annoyed by the racism of Boston printers, the book's London publication made Phillis's work even more prestigious.[10]

Henry Louis Gates Jr. notes, "Everyone knew that the

publication of Wheatley's book was an historical event,
greeted by something akin to the shock of cloning a
sheep." Even the printer, Archibald Bell, was quoted in the
*London Morning Post* as saying, "The book here proposed
for publication displays perhaps one of the greatest
instances of pure, unassisted genius, that the world ever
produced."[11]

Unfortunately, the Countess of Huntingdon was too ill
to make the journey from her estate in South Wales to
meet Phillis in London. But she arranged for Phillis to
meet members of the British royalty and other prominent
people, many of whom gave her books as gifts—the first
time Phillis had owned her own books. Phillis was squired
about London by the great Grenville Sharp, who had led
the movement to end slavery in England. The *London
Chronicle* published her poem "Farewell to America,"
written before her departure from Boston and sent to the
newspaper by Susanna Wheatley.

In July, Phillis received word that Susanna was so ill
she needed Phillis to return to Boston. Once again,
newspapers on both sides of the Atlantic noted the
departure of "the extraordinary Poetical genius" and the
"celebrated young negro poetess." If Phillis had stayed in
London, she would have been free. But she assured her
new British friends that the Wheatleys would free her upon
her return. How could they not?[12]

In September 1773, Phillis's book appeared in London.
She was the first African American and the second
American woman (after Anne Bradstreet) to publish a
book. British, Irish, and Scottish newspapers published
reviews and advertisements praising *Poems on Various*

*Subjects, Religious and Moral By Phillis Wheatley, Negro Servant to Mr. John Wheatley, of Boston*, in New England. Some of the reviews "went so far as to indict the rank hypocrisy involved in the likes of such an obviously gifted woman as Phillis being compelled, by force of law, to remain a slave in an avowedly liberty-loving town like Boston."[13]

## Freedom

One newspaper, *The Monthly Review*, was so condemning of Phillis's enslaved status that the Wheatleys did free her when she returned in Boston. While Phillis did continue to live in the Wheatley household to care for Susanna, she wrote to the Rev. Samson Occom in 1773 about how happy she was to be free. He published her letter in several newspapers.

Phillis's books arrived in Boston in December 1773. The *Boston Gazette's* advertisements referred to her now as "Phillis Wheatley, Negro girl," not "servant." As a free woman, Phillis had to rely on book sales for money. She placed ads and signed copies, anticipating pirated versions of her work. The books had taken longer than expected to arrive because the book had gone into his fourth printing in London. But as William Robinson writes, "How much of the sales monies Phillis received from these books—if she received anything—is unknown. The original arrangements gave Phillis 'half the sales of the Books;' the other half of such monies was presumably to be paid to Mr. and Mrs. Wheatley as reimbursement for monies advanced for Phillis' London room and board."[14]

As 1774 opened, Phillis continued to write poems for

people "for hire" and for newspapers. She wrote another letter to Rev. Samson Occom that was a stinging "condemnation of slave-holding ministers and other so-called freedom loving whites." It appeared in local newspapers, and remains "the most forceful of the several anti-slavery remarks that she composed."[15]

When Susanna Wheatley finally died in March, 1774, Phillis was essentially on her own. The arrival of more British troops made Boston a difficult place in which to live. Phillis moved to Providence, Rhode Island, to care for Mary Wheatley Lathrop, the Wheatleys' daughter, who had suffered the deaths of four children and the difficult birth of a fifth.

In October of 1775, Phillis penned a poem of praise to George Washington when he assumed command of the Continental Army in Cambridge. By doing so, Phillis had now publicly aligned herself with the American cause and her letter was published in newspapers and magazines. General Washington responded in February 1776, inviting her to his headquarters. "I shall be happy to see a person so favored by the muses," he wrote. But it is unlikely that Phillis would have risked crossing British lines to visit Cambridge, and there is no evidence that such a meeting took place.

General Washington and his men drove the British out of Boston in March, and Phillis returned to a city of destruction. The Wheatley mansion was ruined, and the exorbitant price of all manner of goods made it impossible for her to sell books. Phillis lived for a time with a niece of Susanna's, and she was dismayed when John Wheatley died in 1778 leaving nothing to her in his will.

## Decline

Phillis decided to look up John Peters, a lawyer and grocer on King Street she had met several years earlier. She lived with him for a while, and they eventually married and moved to a house on Queen Street. William Robinson describes their marriage as "sorry," and John Peters as "seemingly ambitious, vain, wig-wearing, and cane-carrying ... a lawyer, sometimes a journeyman baker, and sometimes a doctor" who had "amassed something of a small fortune early on in his marriage to Phillis." John Peters apparently wanted a more traditional wife, and not a poet.[16]

Phillis was now "grievously disappointed by the pitiful turn of events in her life." She kept writing, but she was unable to earn money from her work. She made several attempts to solicit subscribers for a second book, but she was unsuccessful. Phillis was experiencing a "traumatizing decline from her once enviable cultural and privileged status" combined with the "unfamiliar domestic routines and demands engendered by marriage, [and] the deaths of three children as infants." While no birth or death records of these children have been found, they are mentioned by John Peters in a law suit and by a contemporary account.[17]

After the war ended, John Peters opened a shop on Prince Street, went bankrupt, and was sent to debtors prison. Phillis engaged in domestic work at a boarding house, but she was barely getting by. As poor and ill as she was, Phillis kept writing, hoping for a second chance at success. When the Americans signed a peace treaty with France in 1784, she was able to publish a poem about the event in a local newspaper. In September 1784, the *Boston Magazine* published Phillis's final poem along with a rather desperate advertisement for subscribers to her book.

On December 5, 1784, Phillis Wheatley Peters and her last child died. She was either thirty or thirty-one years old. Her funeral took place in the Todd home near West Boston Street and the Granary Burying Ground, where Susanna Wheatley was buried. It is not known where Phillis was laid to rest. At the time, African Americans in Boston were buried on Copp's Hill in the North End.

John Peters tried to retrieve the manuscript of Phillis's second book from a friend she had shared it with, but he was never able to publish his late wife's work. In 1786, two years after Phillis's death, her first book was reissued in the United States and it has been reprinted more than a dozen times since then.

## Her Faith in Action

Some historians conjecture that Phillis may have been raised in the Moslom faith, considering the part of Africa where she was born. But Phillis adopted Christianity when she was purchased by the Wheatleys.

Susanna Wheatley, Phillis's mistress and a devoted Congregationalist, instructed her daughter, Mary, to teach Phillis how to read and write. The Bible was Phillis's earliest text. There, Phillis learned that she had as much right to God's love and mercy as anyone, that slavery and denying "Negroes" their place in the "angelic train" was wrong, and that anyone, good Christian citizen and minister alike who supported slavery, or who remained silent and complicit, were violating God's law.

These were the days of the Great Awakening, which stressed "conversion through spiritual rebirth and acceptance of Jesus Christ as one's personal savior." When the great evangelical preacher George Whitefield visited Boston, he spoke directly to slaves when he preached and promised them spiritual freedom. As Vincent Carretta explains, "Wheatley was a beneficiary of the Great Awakening, with its Protestant emphases on the need for literacy because of the primacy of the Bible, on the need for spiritual self-reflection and self-assessment, and on the Christian duty to evangelize to white as well as to black audiences. As an enslaved woman, she did not have the opportunity to preach directly, [but she] employed evangelical Christianity as both the means and the end for getting into print."[18]

Phillis wrote with both religious and moral authority. She employed "liberation theology"—meaning, that God favors the oppressed.[19]

In her poem "On Being Brought from Africa to America," she wrote,

'Twas mercy brought me from my pagan land,
Taught my benighted soul to understand
That there's a God—that there's a Saviour too;
Once I redemption neither sought nor knew.
Some view our sable race with scornful eye—
'Their color is a diabolical dye.'
Remember, Christians, Negroes black as Cain
May be refined, and join the angelic train.

In her letter to the Rev. Samson Occom, first published in the March 1, 1774 *Connecticut Gazette*, she wrote a condemnation of the ministers who "countenance and help forward the calamities of their fellow creatures":

"Reverend and honoured Sir,

I have this day received your obliging kind epistle, and am greatly satisfied with your reasons respecting the negroes, and think highly reasonable what you offer in vindication of their natural rights: Those that invade them cannot be insensible that the divine light is chasing away the thick darkness which broods over the land of Africa; and the chaos which has reigned so long, is converting into beautiful order, and reveals more and more clearly the glorious dispensation of civil and religious liberty, which are so inseparably united, that there is little or no enjoyment of one without the other: Otherwise, perhaps, the Israelites had been less solicitous for their freedom from Egyptian slavery; I do not say they would have been contented without it, by no means; for in every human breast God has implanted a principle, which we call—it is impatient of oppression, and pants for deliverance; and by the leave of our modern Egyptians I will assert, that the same principle lives in us. God grant deliverance in his own way and time, and get him honour upon all those whose avarice impels them to countenance and help forward the calamities of their fellow creatures. This I desire not for their hurt, but to convince them of the strange absurdity of their conduct, whose words and actions are so diametrically opposite. How well the cry for liberty, and the reverse disposition for the exercise of oppressive power over others agree—I humbly think it does not require the penetration of a philosopher to determine."

Here, she chastises "good Christians" for holding God's children in bondage:

"But how presumptuous shall we hope to find
Divine acceptance with the Almighty mind
While yet o deed ungenerous they disgrace
And hold in bondage Afric: blameless race
Let virtue reign and then accord our prayers
Be victory ours and generous freedom theirs."

After Phillis was freed, during these days of the Enlightenment, Carretta explains, her religious beliefs and political ideology propelled her forward. Enlightenment philosophy was consistent with "civil and religious liberty" because in both cases there was a natural human urge to be free.[20]

She wrote:

"In every human Breast, God has implanted a Principle, which we call Love of Freedom; it is impatient of Oppression, and pants for Deliverance."

But Phillis didn't just use her Christian principles and imagery to write against slavery. Every one of her poems is filled with Christian themes about life and faith in this world and the next. She believed that life was a stop on the way to heaven, and she used her elegiac poems, in particular, to comfort people. In fact Phillis's religion was a motive for her writing.[21]

One of the reasons Phillis's London publisher insisted on

proof of her literary ability was her facile use of Biblical references and theological understanding. Here is just one example of her active faith, written to the Rev. Dr. Thomas Amory in praise of the role he played in "cultivating" religion "in ev'ry noble mind":

"TO cultivate in ev'ry noble mind
Habitual grace, and sentiments refin'd,
Thus while you strive to mend the human heart,
Thus while the heav'nly precepts you impart,
O may each bosom catch the sacred fire,
And youthful minds to Virtue's throne aspire!
When God's eternal ways you set in sight,
And Virtue shines in all her native light,
In vain would Vice her works in night conceal,
For Wisdom's eye pervades the sable veil.
Artists may paint the sun's effulgent rays,
But Amory's pen the brighter God displays:
While his great works in Amory's pages shine,
And while he proves his essence all divine,
The Atheist sure no more can boast aloud
Of chance, or nature, and exclude the God;
As if the clay without the potter's aid
Should rise in various forms, and shapes self-made,
Or worlds above with orb o'er orb profound
Self-mov'd could run the everlasting round.
It cannot be--unerring Wisdom guides
With eye propitious, and o'er all presides.
Still prosper, Amory! still may'st thou receive
The warmest blessings which a muse can give,
And when this transitory state is o'er,
When kingdoms fall, and fleeting Fame's no more,
May Amory triumph in immortal fame,
A nobler title, and superior name!"

Finally, Phillis's faith in action shows in the fact that even in the midst of extreme poverty during her years with John Peters, she was still planning her second book of poems, religious and moral, meant to inform and inspire.

## Sites to Visit in Massachusetts

Old South Meeting House
310 Washington Street
Boston, MA 02110
*Old South has a wonderful exhibit about, and a statue of, Phillis Wheatley. She was a member here.*

Landing Place
Beach and Tyler Streets
Boston, MA 02111
*This is the site of the wharf where the slave ship* Phillis *docked.*

Boston Women's Memorial
Commonwealth Avenue Mall at Gloucester Street
Boston, MA 02116
*The Memorial features Abigail Adams, Lucy Stone, and Phillis Wheatley.*

## Resources

*Phillis Wheatley: Biography of a Genius in Bondage* by Vincent Carretta (University of Georgia Press, 2011).

*The Trials of Phillis Wheatley and Her Encounters with the Founding Fathers* by Henry Louis Gates Jr. (Basic Books, 2003).

*Phillis Wheatley: First African-American Poet* by Carol Greene (Children's Press, 1995).

"Phillis Wheatley" by William Henry Robinson in *Phillis Wheatley and the Origins of African American Literature* (Old South Meeting House, 1999).

*Revolutionary Poet* by Maryann N. Weidt and Mary O'Keefe Young (Carolrhoda Books, 1997).

Websites
*Search for Phillis Wheatley at:*
Boston Women's Heritage Trail
Massachusetts Historical Society
Poetry Foundation

## Notes to the Biographical Sketch

1    *Phillis Wheatley: Biography of a Genius in Bondage* by Vincent Carretta (University of Georgia Press, 2011), 5-6; and "Recovering Phillis Wheatley, Recovering Ourselves" by Marilyn Richardson in *Phillis Wheatley and the Origins of African American Literature* (Old South Meeting House, 1999), 7.
2    *Phillis Wheatley and the Origins of African American Literature*, 30.
3    "Phillis Wheatley" by William Henry Robinson in *Phillis Wheatley and the Origins of African American Literature*, 10-11.
4    Robinson, 11.
5    Ibid., 11.
6    *Revolutionary Poet* by Maryann N. Weidt and Mary O'Keefe Young (Carolrhoda Books, 1997), 28.
7    *The Trials of Phillis Wheatley and Her Encounters with the Founding Fathers* by Henry Louis Gates Jr. (Basic Books, 2003), 27.
8    *Phillis Wheatley and the Origins of African American Literature*, 15.
9    Robinson, 15.
10   Ibid., 17.
11   Gates, 32.
12   Robinson, 17.
13   Robinson, 18.
14   Ibid., 19.

15  Ibid., 21.
16  Ibid., 23-4.
17  Ibid., 24, and Carretta, 177.
18  Carretta, 25, 44.
19  Carretta, 159.
20  Ibid., 160.
21  Ibid., 23.
22  Gates, 27.

**To The King's Most Excellent Majesty**
by Phillis Wheatley
(On the repeal of the Stamp Act)

YOUR subjects hope, dread Sire--
The crown upon your brows may flourish long,
And that your arm may in your God be strong!
O may your sceptre num'rous nations sway,
And all with love and readiness obey!
But how shall we the British king reward!
Rule thou in peace, our father, and our lord!
Midst the remembrance of thy favours past,
The meanest peasants most admire the last*
May George, beloved by all the nations round,
Live with heav'ns choicest constant blessings crown'd!
Great God, direct, and guard him from on high,
And from his head let ev'ry evil fly!
And may each clime with equal gladness see
A monarch's smile can set his subjects free!

"We Believe in You!"  — Bonnie Hurd Smith and HistorySmiths.com

# "Conversations" with the Twelve Women

## Women's Wisdom from the Ages

---

**Here's where it gets fun.**

What can we learn from these twelve women?

You just read their stories, and I hope you came away feeling, as I do, that they are very much "present" in our lives today because they all helped us get to where we are.

Wouldn't it be fun if we could sit down with each one and ask: What advice would you give us today, right now, to guide us in our personal and professional lives—which are, of course, irrevocably intertwined?

This is where "history" really comes to life. Smart is smart. Success is success. Things like technology may change over time, but the fundamental principles of human existence and conducting business really don't.

And here's a quick story to illustrate my point.

I recently led a walking tour in downtown Boston for Simmons College as part of an international conference of women economists. It was a hot, humid, July Saturday

---

morning, and we were inundated by the sounds of traffic, jack hammers, and crowds of tourists and shoppers.

When I first met my tour group of about twenty-five women, I was struck by the fact that only one of them spoke English as her native language—and she was from New Zealand. Every other woman hailed from parts of Africa, Asia, or the Middle East. Despite the challenging conditions of weather and noise, I led them past sites having to do with abolition, woman suffrage, and women's advancements in education, politics, and the law.

The women peppered me with questions about tactics, the role of city, state and federal government, access to education and funding, threats to their work and person— you name it. And it suddenly dawned on me that in some cases I was speaking to the Lucy Stones of their country. The Maria Baldwins. The Lydia Maria Childs. It was a very emotional experience for both sides, I will tell you, because I got it, and they knew I had.

They wanted to learn everything they could about the women we were "visiting" because the women's stories gave them ideas and solutions to the challenges they faced in their own country. In many cases, the challenges here and there, then and now, were the same.

THAT is why it is so important to tell the stories of American women who defied the odds, overcame obstacles, and made the world better. They are not "dead." Not by a long shot. They continue to inspire and inform women throughout the world, and we need to know them better here in America so they can inspire and inform US!

I like to call this section "Women's Wisdom from the Ages." What can the twelve women in this book teach us? How would they advise us?

I imagine these conversations taking place toward the end of their lives, after the women had achieved what they did and now had the time to sit quietly and reflect. Here's what I would report back to you, dear reader, after interviewing each one.

---

### Abigail Adams

I imagine meeting Abigail at her beautiful country home in Braintree, Massachusetts, surrounded by fields, orchards, livestock, and men working the farm she managed so successfully. Abigail spent several years "improving" the home she and John called the "Old House" at "Peace Field," adding rooms, raising ceilings, furnishing it with family pieces and items purchased in Boston and Europe. The Adams Homestead was (and still is) a loving, comfortable, welcoming place for family members and guests.

In the summer, Abigail might have met with me in her flower garden, or on her shady front porch. In the spring, fall, or winter, she would have seated me in the formal parlor near a blazing fire.

"Mrs. Adams," I would have asked, "looking back on your remarkable life and accomplishments, what advice would you offer women today?" Here's how I imagine she would respond.

**"It's not all about you."**
"Hang tough," to use my words, because there are
times when we are all called to a higher purpose
and we need to put the mission first. Abigail endured
John's lengthy absences because he was engaged in
essential, important, and patriotic work. Thanks to David
McCullough's biography of John Adams, we now know just
what a key role he played.

**"Be who you are."**
Abigail was always herself—on the farm or in European
courts. She knew her values. She knew what mattered.
She had the strength of character to be unswayed by
flattery or finery. Part of who she was, was a true partner
to her husband at a time when equality in marriage was
hardly the norm. She managed the family farm to support
his political career. She was his "eyes and ears" back
home. She was his political adviser. There's a reason
she was called "Mrs. President!"

**"Know what and who you stand for
and be prepared to defend it."**
In America, Abigail often had to defend John, first when
he defended the British troops after the so-called Boston
Massacre and, later, when he became president and
negotiated his way out of another war with France and
Britain. In Europe, she defended America. Even later, she
had to defend her son John Quincy Adams as his political
career became more and more prominent. I cannot
imagine Abigail flinching for a second when called upon
to defend principles or the people she believed in.

**"Be creative, and find ways around obstacles."**
During the Revolutionary War, Abigail was really

"up against it" when it came to shortages of money and supplies. In John's absence, she just had to figure things out—and she did. In New York, Philadelphia, and Washington, D.C., same thing. With each new experience came challenges she used her creativity and smarts to find ways around obstacles.

**"Don't be afraid of hard work, but also 'work smart.'"**
No one worked harder on the farm, in person or long distance, than Abigail. And it paid off. She managed a very successful farm, as well as her duties as an ambassador's wife and then as Second Lady and First Lady. Abigail was practical, and focused on what was important. Today, we would credit her with paying attention to the highest ROI (return on investment).

**"When you're called upon to provide leadership, step up."**
Abigail was a long way from rural Weymouth, Massachusetts, when she became the wife of an ambassador in London and Paris, but she stepped up and held her own. She was expected to entertain, maintain standards, and represent America. When she and John returned to the United States, she defined the role of Second Lady, expanded the role of First Lady, and was the first First Lady to live in the President's House in Washington, D.C. She also showed leadership when she famously asked the men in Philadelphia to "remember the ladies." They should have listened!

**"Know that you are influencing the next generation, and take that responsibility very seriously."**
In Abigail's case, that meant educating her children very, very well, and many historians agree that John Quincy

Adams was America's most brilliant president. Abigail not only nurtured him through his early years, but she served as his valued adviser during his career.

_____

### Louisa May Alcott

Louisa May Alcott spent her final days at a convalescent home in Roxbury, Massachusetts, not feeling well at all. I prefer to imagine meeting her in Boston, at her elegant townhouse on Beacon Hill. There, she would have risen to the occasion and, I think, offered us the following advice based on her incredible success.

**"Figure out what you're good at and do it."**
Louisa recalled playing with her father's books as a very young girl, using them as building blocks before she could read or write. Once she could write, it was clear to her that she had found her calling. She never stopped, publishing her first story at age sixteen.

**"Don't let anyone convince you that you can't do something."**
The Boston publisher James T. Fields, editor of _The Atlantic_ magazine, once instructed Louisa's father, "Tell Louisa to stick to her teaching; she can never succeed as a writer." This message ... made her exclaim to her father: "Tell him I will succeed as a writer, and some day I shall write for the Atlantic!" A short time later, she was proven right—and made $50.

**"Be yourself."**
Louisa lived during a time when women had very prescribed roles. She shunned them and "did her own

thing." She had a very strong will, a drive to succeed, and enormous talent. She also had deep faith in God, and knew she had the obligation to use the gifts she had been given.

### "Have courage, and be a leader."

It takes guts to go against the grain, but if you have to, you have to. Louisa not only made more money than most women during her time, she was also an abolitionist, suffragist, and supporter of women's rights. Alcott was the first woman to register to vote in Concord, in the town's election for school committee, and organized other women to follow her lead. In her own family, Louisa had to take the place of her father as bread winner. That took guts.

### "In low moments, just keep going."

Louisa struggled with poverty, overwork, depression, and early professional rejection, even contemplating suicide at one point. But she kept going.

### "Do the right thing."

Louisa was scrupulously honest, direct, caring, and empathetic. She had grown up in an impoverished household, and always felt particularly sympathetic to the poor. She was always generous with her time and her money. Her support of the anti-slavery and women's rights movements were the right thing to do, as was her service as a nurse during the Civil War. She was endlessly giving and loving toward her family—mother, father, three sisters, later nephews and nieces—as well as family friends. If any of them needed her help, she was there. Examples of her generosity abound.

### "Use your network."

Louisa had the enviable good luck to grow up in the company of (the much older) Ralph Waldo Emerson and Henry David Thoreau. Emerson let her use his library. Her father, while never able to support his family, was nonetheless highly regarded by Emerson and many others as a brilliant and progressive teacher and philosopher. She knew or was related to dozens more educated, well connected women and men. All of them supported her, encouraged her, and helped further her success.

### "Associate with the right people."

Louisa's association with Emerson, Thoreau and others in Concord boosted her reputation. Her friendships with such women's rights advocates as Lucy Stone and Edna Dow Cheney did as well. Similarly, she knew all of the important Garrisonian abolitionists including Lucretia Mott, Lydia Maria Child, Wendell Phillips, and more. All of these people lifted her up. She was in very high level company—and they with her.

### "Protect your image and reputation."

Once you achieve success, this is important. Louisa was very concerned about what people said or wrote about her. She chose which images of her were to be used for publication. When she began to achieve a modest level of fame and people asked to write about her, she supplied what information she wished to release to the public.

### "Insist on being paid well, and make money."

Louisa knew well the stilting pain of poverty, and one's inability to act or help others without it. Even as a girl, she was determined to raise her family out of poverty, and especially to relieve her mother of the endless hard work that defined her life. With money, Louisa accomplished her goal. She helped her family in many other ways as well, including purchasing a home for her sister and aging mother, later, for her ailing father in Boston, and the list goes on. Louisa always insisted on being paid what a man would be paid, and she was never refused.

### "Establish boundaries once you are famous."
Louisa detested the streams of "lion hunters," as she called them, who invaded her home and her privacy in Concord to catch a glimpse, secure an autograph, or ask for a photograph. She once wrote to a family friend, "I wish you would write an article on the rights of authors, & try to make the public see that the books belong to them but not the peace, time, comfort and lives of the writers. It is a new kind of slavery."

### "If you are a writer, keep writing until you find your niche."
Some of Louisa's earliest stories were what she called "blood and thunder" tales along the lines of Nathaniel Hawthorne and Edgar Alan Poe. She wrote the stories to make money, and she did, but this style was not her niche. Coaches today would tell you that you can always "course correct," but something has to be set in motion first.

### "Write what you know."
Writers are told this all the time. Part of Louisa's phenomenal success with *Little Women* was because she wrote about her own family life in Concord. Readers of all ages, but especially young people, were drawn to the story because it was, essentially, real. She would also advise you to think about a theme around which you can publish multiple stories or books. *Little Women* didn't end

there. Alcott published several more books that continued the story and each one was a best seller.

**"Once you have found your niche, don't stop."**
Biographers describe Louisa's life as pre-*Little Women* and post-*Little Women*. Once she had found her niche, almost all of the writing she produced until the end of her life was for young people. People called her the "Children's Friend" and the "darling of all American nurseries." Louisa's friend, Mary Bartol, described Louisa, a former teacher, in an article she published after her friend's death: "She talks to girls and boys on their own plane of life, colored with the robustness of sports and strength, and while she grasps their hands, she holds before them a lofty ideal. It is no wonder that they flocked into her presence, whenever they had the opportunity."

**"Enjoy your success, and be happy."**
This did not always come easily for Louisa, but she did travel to Europe and enjoyed the company of her family and close friends. She had known poverty, loss, and illness, and those feelings never quite left her. Her service during the Civil War resulted in a severe case of typhoid from which she never fully recovered. Nevertheless, Louisa was consistently described by her friends as witty and humorous. She would be the first to say, be grateful for your success and enjoy its rewards.

---

### Anne Bradstreet

If we were to meet Anne toward the end of her life at her spacious home in North Andover, perhaps as she was correcting her book for a second publication, what would she say to us as women artists? Unlike women two hundred years later, Anne was charting new territory simply by engaging in the act of writing for publication. She really blazed this trail.

### "Surround yourself with people who support you."

Anne was lucky to have her husband and family support her writing because it was, literally, dangerous for her to write. Women were (supposedly) incapable intellectually, and it was dangerous for women's health to engage in such activity. Anne could have been accused of abandoning her family, and dismissing the accepted patriarchal order of things determined by God. She and her family could have been ostracized, banished, or worse.

### "Surround yourself with people who challenge you."

Anne always had an older, well educated man in her life who challenged her intellectually and theologically. As a girl, her father, Thomas Dudley, and her minister, John Cotton, played this role. Later, in Ipswich, she sought out the company (and library) of Nathaniel Ward. In Andover, albeit briefly, Anne spent time with her brother-in-law, John Woodbridge. It is unclear how much her husband, Simon, challenged her, but they were certainly attracted to each others' minds early on. As it was, once they arrived in Massachusetts, he was frequently away on business.

### "If you need a resource that is not readily available, find it."

Anne found people who had books she could use for her research. Her poems were always grounded in historical and theological scholarship.

**"Carve out time for your art."**
Anne used to write late at night when everyone else was asleep. It was the only time she had privacy and space for her creative thoughts. We all need these moments, regardless of the work we do. We need to value ourselves enough to find the time and the physical space to create.

**"Believe that there is a purpose for you to follow, regardless of what others tell you or 'evidence' to the contrary."**
It really is extraordinary for a seventeenth-century colonial woman to pick up her pen and become the voice of a new country—and America's first published poet. There was nothing and no one to support such a crazy notion. And yet, it was inside of her to do. Anne makes it clear in her writing that she felt pulled forward by a higher power. For her it would have been sinful to deny her God-given gifts regardless of what anyone else thought or expected.

———————

### Lydia Maria Francis Child

At the end of her life, Maria lived in her father's colonial style home in rural Wayland, Massachusetts. I imagine meeting with her many years after her husband's death, and after a long lifetime of courageous accomplishment. How would she advise us?

**"Know what you stand for, and have the courage to defend it."**
In Maria's case, she lived at a time of extreme social upheaval and it took great courage, especially for a woman, to stand up and be counted.

**"Play to your strengths."**
In Maria's case her strength was her writing, and she used her talents brilliantly to further her causes. She was not a particularly good speaker, nor a skilled organizer as others were. She stuck to what she was good at.

**"Never stop educating yourself."**
Especially if you're a writer who people view as an expert on a particular subject, you must keep up with "the latest" and constantly expand your knowledge.

**"Establish a strong support system."**
Especially if you are going to express controversial views, you must have people around you who will support and defend you. This can also mean creating organizations to support your cause. You don't want to be "out there" alone.

**"Learn how to use the media."**
Maria published dozens of articles in the *Liberator* and *New-York Tribune*, two widely read newspapers, as well as numerous political pamphlets.

**"Associate yourself with the right people."**
Maria's support system included William Lloyd Garrison, Maria Weston Chapman, and others who formed Boston's impressive social reform community.

**"Be generous."**
Thanks to Maria Chapman, Harriet Jacobs was able to publish the account of her experience as a "slave girl."

**"Be open minded to other ideas."**
Maria was a lifelong student of world religions, and she

preached and lived tolerance.

### "Watch over your own finances."
David Child, Maria's husband, was constantly in debt or terminating failed business attempts. She often had to lend him money to bail them out.

---

### Margaret Fuller

Because Margaret's life was so tragically cut short, I wouldn't have had the chance to sit down with her late in life. Still, by the age of forty, when she died, she had accomplished a tremendous amount. If I could have met up with her in New York, before she departed for Europe, here's what I think she would advise us.

### "Network and ask for help."
Margaret Fuller grew up in Cambridge, Massachusetts, at a very "heady" time intellectually and philosophically. Young students at Harvard were questioning everything, and some of them were her friends. They had all discovered the German philosopher Goethe, and would soon all be caught up in Transcendentalism. Because of these friendships, she met Ralph Waldo Emerson and became the first editor of the *Dial*, the Transcendentalist newspaper. Because of her young Harvard friend James Freeman Clarke, she published her first essay. Her writing caught the attention of Horace Greeley, the editor of the *New-York Tribune*, and she was "launched" internationally." So... network and ask for help! You have no idea what will lead where.

**"Pay attention, do the research, find information."**
You wouldn't be doing what you do if you didn't care about it. Margaret Fuller's business, through her writing, was to improve the status of women. She was relentless in her pursuit of information about women from different classes, cultures, and parts of the country. As a result, she had an authentic voice that people trusted when she sat down to write.

I think that same lesson holds true for any of us today. Authenticity and trust are critical to any business, and that MUST come through in our marketing, PR, community outreach—everything.

**"Tell the truth."**
Same thing. Aren't we all exhausted by people in business who don't tell the truth? Margaret Fuller was incredibly gutsy for a woman in the nineteenth century to write what she did, but she knew she had to because no one else was. This is probably more of an extreme example than necessary for your business or organization, but maybe not. Whatever business you're in, have the guts to tell the truth to your clients!

**"Show up."**
One of the things about Margaret Fuller that impresses me to no end is the extent to which she "showed up" to find out how women were doing. She went out West to live with "pioneer" women from the East and with Native Americans. She visited prisons in New York, and poor houses, and hospitals. She looked closely at slavery from a woman's perspective. Before she wrote her book, *Woman in the Nineteenth Century*, she had talked to a whole lot of women from many walks of life.

Today, it's so easy to stay in the office and on the computer. But showing up where it matters to our industry and what we care about is important.

**"Enjoy being of service."**
That really is why we are all here. It's when we are at our best, and the magic happens when that service becomes clear and we're doing it.

In Margaret Fuller's case—again, a "mere" woman in the nineteenth century—the question of her service, or purpose, plagued her well into her twenties. She had a breakdown at the time because her father (and teacher, mentor, and champion) died suddenly, and as the oldest child she knew she would have to take care of the family. Deeply depressed, she eventually pulled herself out and wrote in a letter to her brother, "God must have something for me to do."

Well, yes, like change the world. Once she did figure out what she was supposed to be doing, her life and business took off like a rocket. Again, perhaps this is an extreme example, but maybe not.

**"Insist on being paid well. Please!"**
Margaret Fuller had a tough time with this one, partly because of the times. Money was always a struggle, but Horace Greeley at the *New-York Tribune* paid her the same salary as a man's—which was unheard of at the time. Margaret would not want you to go through what she went through, including a period of homelessness, so she would want you to be paid well—especially if you are a woman!

---

### Edmonia Lewis

I think about meeting with her in Rome, before she moved to London at the end of her life. Rome was where she felt at home, free from American racism and sexism. In Rome, she was happy, successful, surrounded by magnificent art, history, and friends. How would she advise us?

**"Just stand."**
As I once heard the actress Cicely Tyson say in a talk about her own life, in the face of racism sometimes you need to "just stand," meaning, be who you are and don't flinch. If seems that there is nothing else you can do, "just stand." That in itself is an act of courage.

**"Use your gifts to their fullest."**
Despite the obstacles of gender, race, and the loss of parents at a young age, Edmonia Lewis knew what her gifts were, she honed them, and used them.

**"Believe in yourself, even if others don't."**
While Edmonia's mother had been an artist of traditional Native American crafts, there is no way in the world anyone would have believed that Edmonia could become the great sculptor she became. There was no precedent for it, and strong messages that she wasn't capable because of her race and her gender. But this is where her faith came into play. She knew what was true, and she believed.

**"Follow your heart."**
Edmonia followed her heart first by studying art at Oberlin, then by asking her brother to help her move to Boston to study sculpture, then by moving to Rome and maintaining

a studio on each continent. She also followed her heart by using her art to express the political and religious themes she cared so much about.

### "Be careful whom you trust."
As a trail blazer, and as a woman of color, people were not always on Edmonia's side. She had to be careful, as does anyone who achieves fame, fortune, or who stands out.

### "Consider your environment (place and people)."
You won't do your best work in a place where you don't feel safe and respected. In Edmonia's case, she had to move to Rome to escape the crushing racism and sexism of Boston and the United States that could have kept her from realizing her potential.

### "Never underestimate the power of art to change public opinion."
Edmonia Lewis sold hundreds of copies of her political sculptures, especially her portraits of John Brown and Charles Sumner. People were moved by them.

### "Find out what people are interested in."
Without compromising your integrity, can you create products that people will love and then duplicate them? Edmonia made lots of money doing that!

### "Be very image conscious."
A shroud of mystery never hurts. Edmonia's background was never clear and she liked it that way. She fascinated people. It probably helped sales!

### "Learn how to work the media."
Edmonia often had herself photographed with her work to

reinforce her cultural background and remind people that African Americans and Native Americans could, indeed, be great sculptors and artists. Again, she was always conscious of how her image was portrayed.

### "Self-promote!"
If you don't sell yourself, you won't get business! Edmonia was a genius about using the media and her contacts to further her career.

_____

### Judith Sargent Murray

Before Judith moved to Natchez, Mississippi, in 1818, I can picture meeting with her in her townhouse at Franklin Place in Boston. She would have been sixty-seven years old, and accutely aware of her successes and impact because of the young people who continued to surround her. What would she tell us?

### "Reverence yourself."
This is a direct quote from Judith, and a recurring theme in her essays. She was very concerned about girls' self-esteem and encouraging parents to do better in this area. She believed strongly in "female abilities," and wanted us to believe in ourselves.

### "Never stop educating yourself."
Judith began a life-long process of self-education at a very young age, and she never stopped. As a girl in the eighteenth century, she was denied the education her brother Winthrop received to prepare him for Harvard College. But she did make use of the family library, and became a life-long student of the humanities.

### "Don't listen to public criticism."

She got a lot! And while some of it was wounding, Judith carried on. She had a strong sense of her gifts, purpose, and ability to impact the next generations. Her faith certainly played a role here. Why would God have given her talents, drive, and opportunity if she wasn't supposed to use them?

### "Manage your money wisely."

In Judith's time, women weren't always able to make decisions about their money. This was something she wrote about quite a bit in her essays. But where she could, and especially when she was married to John Murray who traveled frequently, she was very careful with what she had. Despite the fact that she was the daughter of a wealthy family, Judith struggled with money throughout her adult life.

### "Know that you are responsible for yourself."

If you're lucky enough to find the right marriage partner that's terrific, but Judith cautioned that we must be responsible for ourselves either way—including financially. We must never assume or expect someone else to take care of us.

### "Any obstacle in your way because you're a woman is a lie."

Judith devoted her literary career in large part to demonstrating female abilities and convincing women and men that women were "every bit as capable." If women seemed lacking, it was only through "want of education." She overcame many obstacles in her lifetime, one after another, believing in herself and finding a way around.

**"Let your voice be heard."**
Judith was writing at a time when women didn't speak in public. Her powerful voice came through in her writing, and she encouraged the next generation to follow her lead.

**"Write!—and write well!"**
Judith believed so strongly in the power of the written word. It's still true today, even if writing has shifted into electronic formats. And good writing matters. Not texting, not dumbing down. Clear, engaging writing matters.

**"Don't underestimate the role faith can play."**
Judith's faith was integral in everything she throught, did, and wrote. It got her through low moments, and truly inspired her to act. For her, equality was God's plan. Anything in the way of that needed to be challenged.

————————

### Elizabeth Peabody

I would love to visit Elizabeth in Boston, at her home and book store on West Street, where she was the "first" in so many areas—all of them tied to public education.

**"Be yourself and act."**
This is a direct quote from Elizabeth, who famously said, "I must be myself and act." Despite obstacles for women at the time, Elizabeth was always herself and she always acted. As a teacher, writer, editor, publisher, and founder of the kindergarten movement, Elizabeth was tirelessly an educator, always looking for new ways to help and reach people. She was also highly self-

reflective and knew herself well. She was engaged "in an endless quest to take the measure of her interior life," one of her biographers wrote. She even wrote a spiritual autobiography at age twenty-one.

### "Value education in all of its forms."

Being a classroom teacher and founder of the kindergarten movement in America was one way Elizabeth could provide education. She also educated people as a writer, editor, and publisher. Elizabeth placed a very high value on education, for all ages. As she once wrote, education was "the passionate pursuit of my life."

### "Understand that children are unique individuals and treat them with respect."

This was a new concept at the time, promoted especially in Germany, and it formed the basis of Elizabeth's work to found the kindergarten movement in America. It was also what Bronson Alcott believed, whose school she taught in and wrote about, and what other Transcendentalists promoted.

### "Hang out with the right people, network, and support your friends."

Elizabeth was part of the Transcendentalist crowd gathered around Ralph Waldo Emerson, and she derived support and encouragement from them. As the editor of the *Dial*, the Transcendentalist newspaper, as a publisher, and host of Margaret Fuller's "Conversations," she, in turn, was able to help her friends publish their work. Everybody won.

### "Ask questions."

Highly intellectual and curious, Elizabeth rarely

accepted anything at face value. Instead, from the Bible to contemporary writing and discussions, she asked questions. She went so far as to teach herself Hebrew as a girl to be able to read the Bible for herself and not settle for others' interpretations.

**"Set high standards for yourself, and high goals."**
Elizabeth was the first woman publisher in Boston and the founder of the kindergarten movement in America. Just because something hadn't been done before, she was not deterred! She expected a lot of herself, and she followed through.

---

### Sarah Parker Remond

Unless I could travel to Europe, I would have to catch Sarah in between speaking engagements here in the United States! Perhaps I could meet with her in Salem, on a visit to her family home.

**"Believe in your value, despite what others might tell you."**
Sarah lived with the cruelty of racism her entire life, choosing to live in Italy at the end of her life rather than return to the more racist United States. Her mother instilled in her a sense of her self-worth. She saw her father prosper as a business man in Salem despite his race. She also believed that God's law was supreme, and that everyone had been created equal.

**"Play to your strengths."**
As a public speaker, one of Sarah's "unique selling points" was that she was an African American woman. Despite

the novelty of women taking to the public stage, she—and William Lloyd Garrison, who hired her—knew she could appeal to audiences with the moral authority of a woman. She could speak to the issues of rape, family destruction, and terrified children. She could especially reach women on their own level, trusting that they would influence their husbands.

**"When you're called to leadership, step up."**
Ending slavery was a matter of life and death. Sarah knew she had the ability, the support, and the courage to take to the public stage, speak, raise money, and travel. She stepped up.

**"Have courage, knowing that you're doing what you were called to do."**
Sarah displayed enormous courage by speaking from the stage, by committing acts of civil disobedience, by traveling alone, by taking leadership roles in anti-slavery organizations, or by pursuing her education in Europe and becoming a doctor. Truly, she seemed unflinching in the path she was on.

**"Don't let your voice be silenced."**
Not ever.

**"Be aware of your impact and influence."**
Sarah was well aware of her role as a woman and as an African American when it came to breaking down barriers. The newspapers covered her activities and her speeches. People—black and white, male and female—were paying attention. She was very careful about her public image.

**"Write your own story."**

With the media coverage she received over the years, it was very wise of Sarah to write her own autobiography and have it excerpted.

### "Have a strong support system."

Acts of courage, especially when personal safety and public criticism are involved, truly deserve and require a strong support system. Sarah was lucky to have the parents she did, both of them strong, successful, and determined to raise their children with a sense of purpose and high self esteem. From childhood, Sarah was also surrounded by her parents' friends—leading abolitionists, black and white. These friendships endured. Both in the States and in Europe, she made sure to maintain close ties with like-minded people.

### "Be mindful of your environment."

Sarah chose to live in England and then Italy, never returning to the United States, because American racism was so destructive to her well being. In Europe, she could pursue the higher education she so wanted which she could never have received back home. In Italy, she became a doctor and practiced medicine for twenty years. Good for her!

---

### Maria Miller Stewart

I imagine sitting down with Maria Stewart at the Freedmen's Hospital in Washington, D.C. in 1879 where she served as Matron and where she died. She had just reissued her book of essays, adding new material and seeking "endorsements" from "important men" to testify to her abilities—not that she needed it, but this was a tradition among African American writers, especially women. Looking back on her life, what would she advise us?

**"Be fearless."**
I cannot imagine the courage it took for an African American woman to take to the public stage and deliver the first speech in the United States by an American-born woman. But the issue of slavery was too important for her to not speak out. And, she believed to her core that God was with her. Still, imagine all that she risked, physically, socially, and politically.

**"If you see something wrong, don't sit on the sidelines."**
Along the same lines, Maria was well known for her criticisms of anyone who did not speak out against slavery, or work against it, or who were complicit by their silence. These included "good Christians" and ministers. Again, she displayed real courage by taking them on.

**"Use your gifts."**
Knowing that she had the gifts of oratory and writing, Maria spoke from the stage and spoke through newspapers and books.

**"Go where you are needed."**
She took to the public stage, wrote for the *Liberator*, published pamphlets and books, taught school, founded schools, and managed a hospital for freed slaves. Without the benefit of journals and letters, we have no way of knowing (at this time) who she might have impacted in her personal life through counseling or letters.

**"Align yourself with the right people."**
Maria Stewart formed a powerful alliance with William Lloyd Garrison, the editor of the *Liberator* and one of the most influential abolitionists. Earlier, she befriended the great David Walker whose influence on the cause was legendary. He was her intellectual and political mentor.

**"Have mentors and a support system."**
If you are going to put yourself "out there" in the public arena, you need support. Any coach today will tell you this. Maria could count on her mentors, David Walker and William Lloyd Garrison.

**"Never let your voice be silenced."**
She did not let her voice be silenced, both as an African American and as a woman—and people tried for both reasons!

**"Network."**
Maria attended conventions for abolition and women's rights where she was able to be among like-minded people. This is so important to do! You need to know that you're not alone.

————————

### Lucy Stone

How would Lucy Stone advise us? Looking back on an incredibly full and successful life, I envision asking her this question at her home in Dorchester, Massachusetts, while her health still allowed her to respond.

**"Believe in yourself."**
Lucy Stone didn't let her father's low opinion of her stop

her from pursuing an education. Luckily, she had other people in her life who believed in her, and she had faith in herself and in her Creator. She also had a sense of the work she would do in the world because of her exposure, in writing and in person, to other abolitionists and women's rights advocates.

Her faith in herself guided her throughout her life. At college, despite the fact that women did not speak in public at the time, she studied oratory (public speaking) and formed a club to practice. She started publishing controversial essays as a college student. She took to the stage to speak up for women's rights and against slavery. She kept her own name when she married. She started a national newspaper. She sided with Frederick Douglass over African American men's right to vote, even though it meant splitting apart the women's movement. Decision after decision, although oftentimes controversial, seemed to come almost with ease because of her faith in herself and clarity of purpose.

**"Educate yourself."**
Whatever it is that you doing in your cause, business, or organization, learn everything you can about it. Learn who the other players are, what's been done in the past and what needs to be done, where you can plug in, and where you will be effective with your particular talents. Read books, find websites—you need to transform yourself into the expert on your subject. And this work is never done. You should always be learning and growing as you step up more and more into your work.

Lucy Stone never stopped studying, attending events, or discussing ideas with friends, colleagues, or influencers by letter or in person. She was a lifelong student of her two causes because so much was at stake.

### "Determine the right tactics."

If you're attempting to sway public opinion on something you care about (including attracting members or customers), you need to figure out who you need to reach, where those people are, and how to reach them. In the communications profession we would say: Audience, Message, Method. All three need to work in harmony for it to work.

In Lucy Stone's case, she spoke at public events (her own or other people's); met privately with people, including detractors; published and distributed pamphlets and the proceedings of women's rights conventions; wrote newspaper articles; started her own newspaper; and prepared petitions to legislatures. She also showed up at other people's events to make her presence known, thereby publicly endorsing other women's rights advocates and abolitionists.

She also organized. While the first women's rights convention was held in Seneca Falls, New York in 1848, the attendees were mostly local. Lucy Stone helped organize the first national women's rights convention in Worcester, Massachusetts, in 1850, where multiple train lines converged, overnight accommodations were available, the media would show up, and politicians would pay attention. She knew there was strength in numbers, and that a public showing of those numbers would attract others to the cause—and display their seriousness of purpose to opinion leaders and the public.

When the women's movement split over the 14th Amendment in 1869, Lucy Stone's group worked for woman suffrage state-by-state, and embraced working class members and issues as well as those from the middle class. The competing group, headed by Susan B. Anthony and Elizabeth Cady Stanton, focused on a federal Constitutional amendment and its middle class membership. The state approach is what worked many years later.

**"Network, and hang out with likeminded people."**
Lucy Stone's network of friends and colleagues was long and impressive. They gave each other strength, ideas, and support. They learned from each other, and raised each other up. Some of them mentored her, while she mentored others. They were in a constant state of learning and doing.

These are the kinds of people you want to be around! Please don't waste one more second of time with people who don't believe in you, your business, organization, or cause, or who lower you down in any way. These people are draining away your precious time and energy. You need a "tribe" that will support you!

**"Be prepared to make controversial decisions and stand by them."**
When Lucy Stone married Henry Blackwell, she refused to change her last name, thus becoming the first woman in America to keep her own name. (Thereafter, women who followed her lead were called "Lucy Stoners.") She and Henry also read a statement protesting the disturbingly sexist marriage laws at the time. Their vows, and their protest, were published widely. During their years together,

if Lucy Stone had to sign a legal document or register at a hotel, she had to write, "Lucy Stone, married to Henry Blackwell," for her signature to be legal.

The year after she was married, Lucy refused to pay property taxes. She and Henry had kept her house in her name, and she wanted to make the point that this was an appalling example of "taxation without representation." If she couldn't vote, why should she pay taxes?

After the Civil War, when the 15th Amendment to the Constitution was proposed giving the right to vote to all "male citizens," including African American men, the women's movement split in two. The group headed by Susan B. Anthony and Elizabeth Cady Stanton refused to support the amendment because it did not include women. Lucy Stone, Julia Ward Howe, Frederick Douglass, and others believed that it was literally a case of life or death to secure the right to vote for African American. They also believed their efforts would pave the way for woman suffrage. Stone's decision set woman suffrage back by many years, but this was the decision she had to make.

**"Have courage."**
Know that you might be ridiculed, criticized, and possibly even threatened. Decide that you don't care. Protect yourself, but carry on.

In Lucy Stone's case, during her talks, (some) men would hiss at her, throw eggs, threaten to tear apart the stage, or hurl hymnbooks. (Why hymn books? Because she often spoke in churches, where she used her knowledge of Greek and Hebrew to translate the Bible differently— pointing out that the male ministers had gotten things wrong when it came to women's supposed inferiority. Hence, the flying hymn books!)

And yes, it takes huge courage to take on the male ministers. Lucy had been raised in the Congregational church, but was outraged that women weren't accepted as voting members. The church also condemned the abolitionist Grimké sisters, Sarah and Angelina, whose work Lucy so admired. Eventually the Congregational church expelled Lucy for her views, and she joined the much more accepting Unitarian church.

In 1870, Lucy Stone raised money to start a suffrage newspaper called the *Woman's Journal.* It was the year after the split in the woman suffrage movement, and Stone wanted to make sure her group's views were in the public sphere. Yes, she had spoken in public and published articles and pamphlets, but starting a national newspaper and becoming its editor (after Mary Rice Livermore edited it for two years) was quite a courageous endeavor!

**"Know that you will inspire others to join you, and be prepared to give them something to do."** Some people who sign on to your cause or organization will already know how they want to help. They will be self-starters and leaders in their own right, and you will become colleagues. But others may very well contact you to ask, "How can I help?" You need to have answers ready.

These days, anyone with a computer and online access can help you with your newsletter or website. They can forward your news releases or email blasts to their own networks. I'm sure you have a long list of tasks you should delegate to allow you to focus on big picture thinking and activities!

### "Don't let people in your life get in the way."
Women are forever being asked to put aside their own aspirations in favor of a husband, their children, or a sick relative. Lucy Stone really had to be persuaded to get married, and it took Henry Blackwell a long time to persuade her to say "yes." Why? Because almost all of the married women she knew had to put their husbands in first place and set aside their own work. In addition, at the time, marriage laws still favored the husband in all things—property rights, conjugal rights, control over finances, control over the children, you name it. For a woman in the nineteenth century, getting married was a risky proposition. Luckily, Henry supported her work 100%.

As for children, of course their needs come first, and I feel very strongly about that. But that does not mean martyring yourself by putting your work on hold indefinitely. In Lucy Stone's case, she did suspend her public speaking and traveling when her daughter, Alice Stone Blackwell, was born in 1857 (after an infant son had died). But she still found ways to remain active in women's rights, and resumed her work fulltime several years later when her services were needed after the Civil War to help pass the 15th Amendment.

(It should also be noted that Alice Stone Blackwell grew up to become a leader in the suffragist movement, the editor of her mother's newspaper, the *Woman's Journal*, the successful peacemaker between the two hostile sides of the woman suffrage movement, a witness to the passage of woman suffrage in 1920, and the author of a biography of her mother. Clearly, Lucy made the right decision and was a wonderful mother and mentor!)

These are all your personal decisions, of course, given your own situation, including when it comes to the care of sick relatives or tolerating dysfunctional friendships. It's just that historically, women have always been expected to put themselves in second place.

It is NOT selfish to put yourself in first place, even though women are told it is. In fact, as the life and business coach Baeth Davis says, "You cannot be of service to anyone or anything if you are not in service to yourself first." She also says, "Be of service, not in servitude." Again, women are still expected to be in servitude, and that is really not okay!

Even in the nineteenth century, Lucy Stone figured this out and was never in servitude, but happily of service—to her family, and the country.

---

### Phillis Wheatley

This one gets a little complicated, because Phillis's life ended so tragically. Poor, ill, believing herself a failure and dying young, that's not when I'd want to ask her advice about success. In fact, I would love to have two conversations with Phillis—one at the height of her success, and the other at the end of her life about the impact of slavery, racism, and poverty on her final days. Quite a contrast. But, for now, I'd like to meet with her in Boston shortly after the publication of her book.

**"Believe in yourself."**
It is unclear what Phillis's religious life in Africa may have involved, but she embraced Christianity when she lived in Boston and became a member of Old South Meeting House. Her choice of religion aside, what comes through loud and clear in her writing and her actions is a deep faith in God, in God's love for her, and, by extension, faith in herself. Because of this faith, she acted in ways that were completely unexpected of her, especially as an African American woman in eighteenth-century Boston, and she was successful.

**"Surround yourself with people who believe in you."**
There will always be detractors. There will always be moments when we are filled with self-doubt. Phillis had Susanna Wheatley to believe in her, members of the Wheatley family, and others like the Rev. Samson Occom.

**"Have courage."**
Each one of Phillis's poems or open letters was an act of courage for a young slave woman in Boston. The act of publishing a book of poetry was another act of courage. I believe her faith fueled her courage, as well as the sure knowledge that she was living her life purpose—to sway public opinion against slavery, and to prove the abilities of African Americans by example.

**"If people doubt your capabilities, prove them wrong (and enjoy doing it!)."**
Phillis's London publisher doubted her capabilities as an author. The Wheatleys secured the testimony of leading Boston men who interviewed Phillis and confirmed that she was the real thing. Annoying, yes, but part of Phillis must have enjoyed proving the doubters wrong!

**"Seek and accept support to achieve your goal."**
The American ideal of "going it alone" is rubbish. We all have people in our lives who have helped us. As a young slave woman in Boston, Phillis needed Susanna Wheatley's backing to publish her poems and her book. In Phillis's case, she had little recourse, but she accepted Susanna's help and achieved incredible success as a result. Phillis's goal was to have her voice heard, and she achieved it.

**"Use your creativity and your art to help others."**
Phillis's poetry was an important voice in the chorus of voices calling for an immediate end to slavery. And, as Henry Louis Gates Jr. wrote, by publishing her book of poems, Phillis was "essentially … auditioning for the humanity of the entire African people."

**"Speak up for what is unjust."**
Both before and after being freed, Phillis boldly challenged ministers and "good Christians" alike. She could easily have been silenced, jailed, or even killed for it. Yes, she had Susanna Wheatley's protection to a certain extent, but Phillis was challenging powerful, intractable Christian men.

––––––––––

**Amazing advice from these twelve women—
all of it grounded in wisdom and achievement.
All of it applicable to our lives today.**

**But now, let's go one step further and have our
own conversation!**

# A "Conversation" Between You and Me

## Things to Really Think About and Do

Aren't the twelve women amazing? I hope you enjoyed reading about them as much as I enjoyed writing about them.

As you read the advice they had to offer us today, I'm sure you saw a lot of common denominators like having courage, believing in yourself, and securing a strong support system. I hope you were able to find something to apply to your own life. I like to think of women in history as a "vast army of women"—always on our side, always there!

**And that leads me to having a conversation with YOU.**

My thoughts here are grounded in the women's stories, in my own story, and in what I've learned from the coaches I've been studying with for the past few years.

First, I want you to know that I believe in you. That's why the title of the book is what it is. The twelve women did, and so do I!

It has taken me a while to "get there" myself without the support and faith I didn't know I needed. Life's a journey for all of us, and I hope some of these ideas help you avoid what I didn't. So, let's have a conversation here, and let's continue it online through my email list (bonnie@webelieveinyou.com) or my Facebook page. Here goes!

**Be honest with yourself about your "secret thoughts," the things you probably don't tell anyone else that you really want or are.**
I learned this from a business/spiritual coach named David Neagle, one of the amazing coaches I've been studying with. What do you love to do? What are you good at? What do you want? What do you really, really want?

**Make sure you have the support system you need.**
When I was growing up, I didn't. Yes, that was a long time ago, but in my kind of situation "voices" get planted in your head that can take years to shake off. I could not look to my family as a support system, and I figured that out at a very young age. But I also knew that I needed to replace them with other people who could provide the support I needed, and that's what I did. I turned to teachers, the parents of friends, and friends my own age.

I hope the same is not true for you, but it might be. The very people who are "supposed to" support you don't or can't—for whatever reason. Please be honest with yourself. Do you have the love and support you need? If you don't, where can you find it?

And only surround yourself with people who will lift you up and not tear you down. The "tear you down" behavior is not about you anyway. It's about them. Please keep away from such people! Who can you add to your life who will support you?

**Believe in yourself.**
It's not always easy to do, but you must, wherever it comes from—your faith, your intuition, your secret knowledge about yourself that you don't share with anyone else. People will criticize you or make inappropriate suggestions about what you "should do." You need to have an internal anchor that says, "No. I know who I am. I know what I believe. I know what I can do, and what I will do. No." (Why not practice this out loud?)

Whatever your spiritual beliefs, know that you are not in charge and neither is any other human being. A higher power is. You are a child of the Divine. Don't EVER let anyone treat you as less than that. Not ever. Think of having this belief as a protective shield around you at all times!

**Ask for help.**
No one "does it alone" despite the ages-old American myth that says we're all supposed to. We all have help along the way. For one thing, people do like to help others. For another, there's great joy in asking for and receiving help from someone who will share your journey and help you achieve your goals.

These people could be teachers, clergy, or the parents of friends, but as you get older please think seriously about hiring a professional coach. It made an incredible difference in my life, and still is. All of the successful people I know have had a coach at one time or another. It makes a difference to have someone in your life who really "gets" who you are and what you're trying to do —and who has no other agenda except to help you.

It's more important to get things done than it is to tough it out and struggle alone—as I have, for years. Good grief. Life is too short. Ask for help and receive it graciously!

## Acknowledge your gifts, and find a way to put them to use.

This is big. You may be saying to yourself, "I'm not really sure what my gifts are." As David Neagle, says, "Life leaves clues." Pay attention when something goes right in your life. What's going on there? That's where the answer is. Then, what will you do about it? How will you make "it" grow and prosper?

Whatever your beliefs about life purpose and faith, I believe so strongly that we are all here for a reason. Maybe you know the expression "God don't make no trash." Think about that! Why in the world would you or the twelve women we just read about have certain gifts if we were NOT meant to use them? It just doesn't make sense. These women believed they were literally insulting God, or letting down the Divine, if they did not do their best and use their gifts to help others. In my own Unitarian Universalist tradition, that's part of our history—the mutual "deal" we have with our Higher Power. We've been given gifts it is up to us to use. That's not a bad deal!

Think about creating your own, internal "manifesto"— what you want in your life that you may never tell anyone else. It's your internal "code," almost, for what you want to create in the world, as another amazing coach, Baeth Davis, would say. David Neagle takes this a step further by saying, "It's your job to DECIDE. It's not your job to know HOW you will do something. Make the decision, and "how" will be shown to you. Then, you need to embody your own, personal mission statement. You will make changes along the way, and that's as it should be because you will grow, but you need to really "be" who you are and why you're here.

## Be of service to yourself first.
Baeth Davis famously says, "You can't be of service to anyone if you are not in service to yourself first." We women are taught to put everyone else first—family, friends, clients, causes, and organizations. So was I. But in reality, as Baeth would say, "How can you help anyone else if you're broke, homeless, and sick?" The answer is, You can't. What I just described is actually "servitude," not service, as Baeth would say.

We are also taught that putting ourselves first in any way is selfish. In business, we are taught that if we aren't invisible we're showing off. Can you see how that's rubbish? We are leaving money on the table, and denying ourselves a good income by not being "out there." It took me years to figure this out, but I did. I hope you will as well.

And indulge like heck in self-care! You deserve it. One coach I worked with, Debra Woog, says, "There is no better investment you can make than in your own self-care. Honor yourself the way you would anyone else you love. You are worth it!"

## Be here now. Be present.
This is another Baeth-ism. So often, those of us who are dealing with "stuff" find ways to avoid being present. Sometimes it just hurts too much. I get that. Been there. But if you're not truly present, you won't succeed.

Avoidance behavior could include alcohol, drugs, addictive relationships, too much TV or reading … whatever method you use to not be present, please stop! We need you.

### How are you BEING? Who are you being? How are you showing up?

All of the coaches I've studied with say various versions of, "It's not what you're doing, it's who you're being." Think about that! It's heavy! But it's true. How are you treating yourself? How are you treating others? How do you come across? As hurt, angry, frustrated, and otherwise negative? Why would someone want to be around you? And you probably don't like being around yourself! How is your appearance? Do you look like you're taking care of yourself? Really think about this one … It's not about running around and being busy all the time, constantly "doing." That doesn't get you very far. Are you being the best YOU there is, and if not, why not?

### What stops you?

David Neagle has built his whole business around helping people answer this question. What stops you from achieving your goals? Voices in your head that shouldn't be there? Fear of failure? Fear of success? Fear that no one cares about you? He would also tell you that it's your ego's job to stop you, to keep you broke, to have low self esteem, live in fear, play it safe and familiar. Your ego is a formidable beast to battle, but we're not free if "it" wins. This is something you really need to think about so you can take steps to change your situation.

He, and others, would also tell you to burn the bridge to fear. How does it serve you? It doesn't. It stops you. So do excuses and procrastination. Change is scary. So is fear.

But you can learn to move through fear and you'll be happier when you do!

**Nothing is "wrong" with you.**
Women spend far too much time wondering what is "wrong" with them. Why don't we have more money, a happier personal life, or a more fulfilling profession? When I heard the coach Fabienne Frederickson say, "There's nothing 'wrong' with you, there's just something you don't know. So stop saying it," I took great comfort in that. It really shifted my thinking. How often do you beat yourself up about something being wrong with you? Please stop!

And this is why studying women's history can be so uplifting. I'll choose women and money as one example. I can look at my own history, and my family history, and see why this is an issue for me. But if I turn to women's history there are even more answers. Over the years, think about how women have not been allowed to manage or invest money, to earn as much as a man or to be valued for having a high salary. We didn't get here over night! This stuff has been generations in the making. Think about THAT the next time you have an issue with money. It's not to say that we shouldn't accept responsibility for our decisions but, again, attitudes around women and money didn't just appear today!

**Don't play small, think small, or be small.**
Why would you? Sure, some people will try to keep you small. That's their issue. You know who you are, and what you're supposed to be doing. And you know when you're not doing it, when you've limited yourself, or said, "Well, I can't do that because…." There's nothing worse than that gut feeling that tells us we've acted small. What are the

consequences of not understanding who you are, knowing your talents, your purpose, and taking action? The consequences are a very unfulfilling, small, and sad life.

David Neagle would tell you that the difference between human beings and other species is our power to choose. We can create our lives. We can change what we're not happy with because we created it.

## Have courage, and take action.

I don't know about you, but I am so very tired of people who won't speak up or do the right thing. Whatever the situation, and, yes, we all have to choose our battles, silence is complicity. Of course you will run into some trouble. Who cares? Just be prepared for it. Have a savings account if you need to walk away from a job. Be prepared for people to disagree, criticize, or be angry. Again, who cares? Do you really want to go through life being silent and complicit?

It's easy to play it safe, but what's the point? Do you want to look back on your life and say, "Gee I wish I had done that." No, you don't! What's the worst that will happen if you try something new? You might fail. So what? Try again. Someone might criticize you. So what? It doesn't matter what others think. It only matters what you think. Something you need to do might cost you money. So what? There's more to be had. NOT acting with courage and faith isn't a good way to go through life!

In terms of taking action in your business or political life, you do need a plan you can implement. Being "busy" all the time doesn't work for long. Some people call this the "shiny object syndrome." You get so distracted by the latest program, social media tool, or online opportunity, that you run around and don't actually implement anything. This is especially true for entrepreneurs, and this is where a mentor or coach can really help you. Keep things simple, and expand your plan when it makes sense.

## How are you spending your time?
You will never improve your life if you spend all of your time doing the errands, cleaning the house, taking care of yard work, your kids, the administrative work or billing in your business. What can you delegate? No, it doesn't mean you are showing off. It means you value your time.

I learned this from the incredible coach for women entrepreneurs Ali Brown, and it really shifted my thinking. What is your time worth? Pick a number. $50 an hour? $100? More? If you could hire someone to take care of some of your tasks for $20 or $25/hour (and give that person a job), what creative things could you do with that time? Write your book? Start a business? You need to have the time to do what you're best at, and what you're here to do. You are NOT here to do all the cooking, cleaning, and laundry … and there are plenty of people who are just as good as you are at these tasks. Truly! Delegating is empowering. Kendall Summerhawk, a brilliant money coach, says, "You must let go to grow."

## Find a way around obstacles.
Think how often our twelve women bumped up against some kind of obstacle and found a way around it. You can too. What obstacles stand between your goals and you? Money? Time? Personal issues? The way around might not be clear at first, but that's when you ask for help. That's when you need the support of others, including a

mentor or coach.

**No one is responsible for you but you.**
Not a husband or partner, not a parent … no one is in charge of you but you. David Neagle would say, You must accept responsibility for every single thing in your life, good and bad. Every decision, every action, every outcome. The center of your universe is you.

**Your image is key to your success.**
Everything in your personal and professional lives needs to be consistent with how you feel about yourself—how you look, how you dress, how you interact with people, your website, your Facebook page—everything needs to be in alignment. Every time you look in the mirror, walk into a room, or look at your website, I want you to say YES!!! I am awesome! I am me! (Say this out loud too!)

**Does your environment support your success?**
That includes the people in your life, where you live and work—everything. If your environment doesn't support you, you will really struggle. A couple of years ago I had to make the drastic decision to give up my apartment and sleep on some friends' sofa because a man in my building was threatening me. I put up with his behavior for months, and felt afraid every day. My health and business really suffered. It was a terrible decision to have to make—to become homeless because I didn't have the money to find a new apartment—but what a difference it made to feel safe and among friends! Within a couple of months, I did have a new home, and my business turned around.

**Take care of your money.**
Your relationship with money is not your fault. For centuries, women have essentially been brainwashed into thinking that being poor is all they could or should expect. It's a lie. It's been a way to keep us down—and that means keeping us from acting in the world in a big way. It's a lie, and let's stop this together now!

For many women, there's also a direct connection between asking for money and not being able to receive compliments about our work. This needs to stop too! "Your value goes hand in hand with what you think you deserve," Baeth Davis says. Another Baethism is: "You have to feel deserving of success."

**How do you act in business?**
Whether you go into business for yourself or pursue a more traditional career path, know that women and men behave differently in the business world. Men, even today, will still try to tell you to do things their way. Don't listen to them! Listen to successful business women and entrepreneurs instead, because they "get it." (See my Coaching Resources list on page 266 for a list of successful women coaches.)

**Your thoughts?**
If these ideas have resonated with you, made you think, or brought tears to your eyes, I would love to hear from you. Please drop me an email at bonnie@webelieveinyou.com.

Be well, be strong, get out there, and be fabulous!

—*Bonnie Hurd Smith, Boston's North Shore*

# Coaching Resources

In the "Conversation Between You and Me" and "Coaching Shorts" sections I quote all of these people. I have learned so much from each one. Check them out!

And please be in touch through the special web page I set up just for you. I would love to hear your comments and suggestions. I also have a special gift for readers that you can download from that page.

**https://historysmiths.com/We_Believe**

## BUSINESS/SPIRITUAL/LIFE COACHES

### Ali Brown
Ali is the leading mentor for women entrepreneurs and an online marketing genius.
www.alibrown.com

### Baeth Davis
Baeth is a life purpose and business coach who also happens to be a hand analyst. She is the real deal.
www.handanalyst.com
www.yourpurpose.com

### Kendall Summerhawk
Kendall specializes in women and money issues. She's "been there," and really knows what's going.
www.kendallsummerhawk.com

### Christine Kane
Christine helps women transform their lives and their businesses with intention.
www.christinekane.com

### Fabienne Frederickson
Fabienne works with women entrepreneurs to attract high paying clients so they can earn more and work less.
www.clientattraction.com/

### David Neagle
David is a business and spiritual coach who helps you transform your mindset to attract the abundance and fulfilling life we all deserve.
www.davidneagle.com

### Jess Weiner
I didn't quote her, but she's worth knowing about.
Jess is the Global Ambassador for the Dove Self-Esteem Fund, and she's doing some incredibly important work.
www.jessweiner.com

### Coaches in Massachusetts:
Debra Woog
www.connecttwo.com

Sallie Felton
www.salliefeltonlifecoach.com

# Final Thoughts

To tell you the truth, I am much more interested in your final thoughts than I am in mine!

What did you learn?

What inspired you?

What will you "take away" from this book and set into motion in your life?

With this book, I set out to connect the dots between past and present for women in ways we could embrace and apply today. I hope I've done my job.

So, I would love to hear from you!

Just go to: www.https://historysmiths.com/We_Believe and drop me an email! Or go to my "We Believe in You" Facebook page.

Please also contact me if I can speak for your organization, contribute to your newsletter, or reach your friends or audience in some other way.

I appreciate your partnership in this important work.

We're in this together!

—*Bonnie Hurd Smith, Boston's North Shore*

# Index

**KEY ISSUES AND
ORGANIZATIONS**

**PLACES AND SITES TO VISIT**

## Acknowledgements

I debuted this material at the Cambridge Center for Adult Education, Simmons College, First Universalist Church of Essex, Massachusetts, and for the Gordon College Old Town Lecture Series. The feedback from the audiences at each venue confirmed that I was on the right track and had something valuable to offer. Thank you!

I'd also like to acknowledge the ongoing support I receive from Laurie Crumpacker of Simmons College, my former professor of women's studies and history many, many years ago, now, the Dean of Arts and Sciences.

Thanks go to the Ipswich Writers Group who listened to my introduction and made some wonderful suggestions...

...to the staff of the Ipswich Public Library for being so welcoming when I used their beautiful space for writing...

...to all of my friends, colleagues, and supporters who ordered a pre-publication copy of the book...

...to all of the Unitarian Universalist ministers who have invited me to speak in their pulpits with passion and purpose...

...to all of the venues who have invited me to speak over the  years...

...and to all of the members of my audiences who have been attentive, interested, and entertained.

Thank you, all! We're in this together. —*Bonnie*

# Believe!

https:historysmiths.com/We_Believe

bonnie@webelieveinyou.com

Like us on Facebook!

27572715R00162

Made in the USA
Charleston, SC
15 March 2014